STUDENT UNIT GUIDE

NEW EDITION

Edexcel A2 Government & Politics

Unit 4C

Governing the USA

Jonathan Vickery

Series editor: Eric Magee

PHILIP ALLAN

Philip Allan Updates, an imprint of Hodder Education, an Hachette UK company, Market Place, Deddington, Oxfordshire OX15 OSE

Orders
Bookpoint Ltd, 130 Milton Park, Abingdon, Oxfordshire OX14 4SB
tel: 01235 827827
fax: 01235 400401
e-mail: education@bookpoint.co.uk
Lines are open 9.00 a.m.–5.00 p.m., Monday to Saturday, with a 24-hour message answering service. You can also order through the Philip Allan Updates website: www.philipallan.co.uk

ISBN 978-1-4441-5301-9

First printed 2012
Impression number 5 4 3 2
Year 2016 2015 2014 2013 2012

Cover photo: Ingo Bartussek/Fotolia

Typeset by Integra, India

Printed in Dubai

Hachette UK's policy is to use papers that are natural, renewable and recyclable products and made from wood grown in sustainable forests. The logging and manufacturing processes are expected to conform to the environmental regulations of the country of origin.

P1991

Contents

Content guidance

Questions & Answers

Getting the most from this book

Examiner tips
Advice from the examiner on key points in the text to help you learn and recall unit content, avoid pitfalls, and polish your exam technique in order to boost your grade.

Knowledge check
Rapid-fire questions throughout the Content guidance section to check your understanding.

Knowledge check answers
1 Turn to the back of the book for the Knowledge check answers.

Summary

Summaries
● Each core topic is rounded off by a bullet-list summary for quick-check reference of what you need to know.

Questions & Answers

Exam-style questions

Examiner comments on the questions
Tips on what you need to do to gain full marks, indicated by the icon e.

Sample student answers
Practise the questions, then look at the student answers that follow each set of questions.

Examiner commentary on sample student answers
Find out how many marks each answer would be awarded in the exam and then read the examiner comments (preceded by the icon e) following each student answer. Some comments include annotations that link back to points made in the student answers, to show exactly how and where marks are gained or lost.

About this book

This guide is designed to help you revise for Unit 4C Governing the USA for the Edexcel Advanced (A2) GCE in Government and Politics. This unit looks at the constitution and institutions of the USA, and considers the extent to which they combine to create an effective, representative and just system of government.

The specification

The four topic areas of Unit 4C are set out below:

Topic	Key coverage
Constitution	• A knowledge of the nature and principles of the US Constitution • An awareness of the constitutional framework within which US institutions operate and of the relationship between the constitution and practical politics • Constitutional rights and an evaluation of their effectiveness
Congress	• A knowledge of the structure and workings of Congress, of the distribution of power within Congress, and of debates about the adequacy of its representative role • A knowledge of factors influencing the relationship between Congress and the presidency, and an ability to discuss the policy significance and institutional effectiveness of Congress • An awareness of the extent and significance of party allegiance
Presidency	• A knowledge of the formal and informal sources of presidential power and of the relationships between the presidency and other institutions • An awareness of the factors that affect the role of the presidency and an ability to evaluate the capacity to provide leadership of the presidency and of recent presidents
Supreme Court	• A knowledge of the composition and role of the Supreme Court • A knowledge of the process for appointing federal judges and of debates about the political significance of the Supreme Court and its impact on public policy in the USA

The **Content guidance** section summarises the essential information of Unit 4C, and includes a range of key terms and a series of examiner tips, which should help channel your revision into the right areas. You will also find a series of knowledge checks, inviting you to test various aspects of your knowledge. The knowledge checks are numbered and at the end of the guide there are suggested answers.

The **Questions & Answers** section includes sample short-answer and essay questions, across all four topics, which are designed to show different levels of achievement. Each answer is followed by an examiner commentary, which points out what has been done well, as well as ways in which the answer could be improved.

Content guidance

The constitution

The key issues addressed in this section are:
- the historical background to the constitution
- the structure of the constitution
- the principles of the constitution
- amendment of the constitution
- the evolution of federalism
- assessment of the constitution

The American Constitution occupies a place in American national life which is almost unimaginable in the UK, and indeed most other countries. It is at the same time a source of national pride and identity, and the defining influence on every aspect of American political life. Politicians will frequently invoke the values of the constitution, and compete with each other to claim more faithful adherence; in a gesture of symbolic fidelity, the first act of the new Republican House of 2011–13 was to read the document aloud in its entirety on the floor of the chamber.

Historical background to the constitution

The constitution was drawn up at the Constitutional Convention of 1787. Before the American Revolution in the 1770s, America was a British colony, and the revolution had its origins in what the colonists saw as the oppressive behaviour of the British government. Their discontent culminated in the Declaration of Independence in 1776, which rejected the British monarchy and Parliament, and claimed the sovereignty of a new nation.

The Articles of Confederation

The first attempt at a US Constitution was the Articles of Confederation drawn up in 1776, and passed in 1777 by the Second Continental Congress, the national representative body. The history of arbitrary British rule and consequent suspicion of centralised authority meant that the primary aim of the Articles of Confederation was to protect the rights of the 13 states, and create only a very weak national government. The national legislature, to be known as the Congress of the Confederation, was to consist of one chamber in which members served one, 1-year term. There was no national executive or judicial branch, and the Congress had no enforceable powers of taxation; any legislative action it took required the approval of a minimum of nine of the 13 state delegations.

In the years that followed, with no sustainable source of income, the federal government struggled to function. Congress was unable to regulate trade, either between the states or

Declaration of Independence
The Declaration of Independence was published on 4 July 1776, asserting the independence of the 13 states. Its second sentence 'We hold these truths to be self-evident, that all men are created equal, that they are endowed by their Creator with certain unalienable Rights, that among these are Life, Liberty and the pursuit of Happiness' has become the defining statement of American values.

with other countries, and commerce suffered. Meanwhile, in the 13 states the suspicion of authority meant that the legislative branches came to dominate; in some states, there was no constitutional provision for a governor at all, and in most the governor was chosen by the legislature. It saw the rise of men who James Madison described as being 'without reading, experience or principle', and who were keen to advance their own interests, often at odds with those of the propertied and moneyed classes.

Knowledge check 1

Who was James Madison?

The Constitutional Convention

The Constitutional Convention took place against the background of these two very contrasting periods of American history; the arbitrary rule of the English had been replaced by a weak federal government and the dominance of the state legislatures, which, in the view of the political establishment at least, was just as bad. The experience of the growing power of the legislatures led Madison to write of them in Federalist Paper 48 that 'it is against the enterprising ambition of this department that the people ought…to exhaust all their precautions.'

Knowledge check 2

What were the Federalist Papers? Why were they important?

Federalists and anti-federalists

The Constitutional Convention was divided mainly between two groups, the federalists and the anti-federalists.

The **federalists** favoured a stronger central government to counter the dangerous tendencies they saw in the state legislatures, and to enable the country to function. Their belief that the views of the common man needed filtering by passing through the medium of a chosen body of citizens 'whose wisdom may best discern the true interest of their country' (Federalist 10) led them to advocate a republican government (an indirect democracy).

In contrast, the **anti-federalists** were hostile to any notion of filtering, which they saw as the elevation of the few at the expense of the many. They believed that representatives should mirror rather than filter public opinion or, preferably, that there should be no representatives at all, and government be conducted through assemblies of the people. Any strengthening of central government at the expense of the states would work against the interests of the majority.

Structure of the constitution

The structure and provisions of the constitution reflect the experience of the two previous periods.

- **Article 1** — Despite the misgivings of the federalists about the power of state legislatures, it was inevitable that the legislature, as the representative body of the people, would have to be pre-eminent. Hence it was accorded the status of Article 1, but its powers were precisely defined, to ensure as far as possible that it did not pose a threat to the entire system.
- **Article 2** — An effective executive branch was seen as vital if the federal government was to succeed and, within the constraints of a constitutional republic, it posed much less of a threat of tyranny than an English monarch, with the consequence that the powers of the office needed to be less closely defined than those of Congress.

- **Article 3** — The judicial branch was famously described by Alexander Hamilton in Federalist 78 as 'the least dangerous' branch, and its power was accordingly even more vaguely defined than the executive's.
- **Article 4** — sets out the relationship between the states to make them more a united whole, and less like independent countries.
- **Article 5** — sets out the process for amending the constitution.
- **Article 6** — confirmed that any state debt already incurred remained valid under the new constitution, and asserted that the constitution and the laws of the United States 'shall be the supreme Law of the Land'.
- **Article 7** — describes the process of ratification.

Knowledge check 3

Which is the longest article of the constitution and why is it the longest?

Principles of the constitution

Republicanism

The republicanism (or indirect democracy) favoured by the federalists was the basis of the system of government, but the methods of election were a compromise with the anti-federalists. Consistent with the anti-federalists' desire for a legislature closely in touch with the views of the people, one chamber was to be elected directly by the people and its members to have a 2-year term of office. However, in keeping with the federalists' distrust of the majority and belief that the popular passions needed to be filtered, only this one chamber, the House of Representatives, was to be directly elected; both the second chamber, the Senate, and the executive, the president, were to be chosen by the state legislatures, the two senators for each state directly, and the president by an electoral college comprised of separate state bodies, chosen as the state legislatures saw fit. Moreover, the members of the Senate were given 6-year periods of office, and only a third were to elected at any one time, further reducing their exposure to any short-term wave of sentiment.

Separation of powers

Madison wrote in Federalist 47 that the accumulation of all power in the same hands 'may justly be pronounced the very definition of tyranny', and consequently each of the three functions of government — legislative, executive and judicial — was to be administered by a separate institution, under the control of different individuals. Thus, members of Congress are forbidden by Article 1, section 6 from being appointed to 'any civil office of Authority of the United States'. In fact, this separation of personnel is not applied completely, and nothing in Articles 2 and 3 prevents a member of the executive branch being a member of the judiciary; for a brief period in 1801, John Marshall was both Chief Justice and Secretary of State.

Examiner tip

The concepts of 'separation of powers' and 'checks and balances' are often confused, so ensure you are clear about the differences between them.

Checks and balances

Given the dangers that legislatures and executives had posed in recent history, checks and balances were incorporated into the powers of both, so that neither should be able to function independently, and each should require the cooperation of the other to carry out its functions; as Madison wrote in Federalist 51, 'Ambition must be made to counteract ambition.'

In addition, Congress was 'internally' checked by being divided into two equal chambers, with different constituencies and terms in office. Thus, Congress has a number of significant checks over the president:

- Congress controls the executive budget.
- Congress can reject all legislation requested by the president.
- Congress can impeach and remove the president for 'high crimes and misdemeanours'.
- The Senate confirms the major presidential appointments by a simple majority.
- The Senate ratifies foreign treaties signed by the president by a two-thirds majority.
- Congress can override a presidential veto by a two-thirds majority in both houses.
- Congress has the sole power to declare war, through a majority vote in both houses.

The president has only one significant check on Congress, the veto of congressional legislation, but given that it impedes Congress carrying out its principal function, it is a significant one.

Furthermore, both branches have a limited check over the judiciary in that:

- the president and the Senate are jointly responsible for judicial appointments
- Congress can decide how many justices sit on the Supreme Court and create new lower courts
- Congress can impeach and remove judges for misbehaviour
- Congress can pass constitutional amendments reversing court decisions

but none is a significant check on the core function of the judiciary.

Federalism

The constitution itself is primarily concerned with the powers and relationships of the different branches of the federal government, and the relationship between the federal government and the states is briefly touched on in Article 6 where, certainly significantly, the supremacy of federal law is asserted. Only in the Bill of Rights, passed shortly after the constitution itself, was it stated in the 10th Amendment that 'The powers not delegated to the United States by the Constitution, nor prohibited by it to the States, are reserved to the States respectively, or to the people', making it explicit that the federal government was entitled to exercise only those powers granted to it by the constitution.

Preservation of individual rights

Again, the preservation of individual rights is not a feature of the original constitution, but is incorporated in the Bill of Rights as a concession to the anti-federalists, reflecting their belief in the need for protection against any form of central government. Thus, the rights contained in the first ten amendments were not originally enforceable against the state governments.

Knowledge check 4

When was the Bill of Rights passed?

Amending the constitution

Procedure

The process for amending the constitution is set out in Article 5 of the constitution.

Amendments can be proposed either by Congress, where they require a two-thirds majority in both houses to be approved, or by a national constitutional convention called by two-thirds of the states. They then need to be ratified either by three-quarters of the state legislatures, or by three-quarters of state constitutional conventions.

The option at both stages of the process of bypassing elected representatives in the legislatures reflects the view of many of the framers that no political authority could be entirely trusted, as perhaps does the exclusion of the president from any part of the process.

All amendments to date have been proposed through the first method of congressional approval and, since it is not specified and it has never been tried (since 1787 at any rate), it is not clear what exactly a national constitutional convention would look like, or how it would be summoned. Successful amendments approved by Congress have then nearly all been ratified by the route of the state legislatures, although state constitutional conventions have been used once, for the ratification of the 21st Amendment.

There is no time limit for the process of ratification stipulated in the constitution; Congress may stipulate a time limit itself but, if none is stipulated, the Supreme Court ruled in *Coleman* v *Miller* (1939) that the process of ratification can be completed decades or even centuries after the original approval by Congress; the 27th Amendment, which was finally ratified in 1992, was approved by Congress in 1789. Whether, if it does set one, Congress can choose to extend the original deadline for ratification, and whether states can rescind their ratification once it has been given, became issues during the attempted ratification of the Equal Rights Amendment during the 1970s. Neither ultimately came to the Supreme Court for decision, and both have still to be resolved conclusively.

History

Only 27 amendments to the constitution have ever been completed. The first ten amendments are collectively known as the Bill of Rights and were ratified by the states in 1791. In the succeeding 220 years, there have been only 17 further amendments, although many thousands have been proposed. All the successful amendments have been concerned either with advancing equal rights or with reforming government structures and practices, with the exception of the 18th and 21st Amendments, which imposed prohibition in 1919 and repealed it in 1933.

Of the many amendments proposed since 1992, none has been approved by the required majorities in Congress, although both the Balanced Budget Amendment in 1995 and the Flag Desecration Amendment in 2006, having passed the House with a two-thirds majority, were only one vote short of two-thirds in the Senate and being sent to the states for ratification.

Given the remote chances of success, it might be wondered why so many amendments *are* proposed. Presidents will sometimes propose amendments to demonstrate their allegiance to their core constituency, knowing nevertheless that they are doomed to failure. President Reagan proposed an amendment reversing the Supreme Court's ruling on school prayers in 1982; although it had a majority in favour, it was 11 votes short of two-thirds in the Senate. President Bush proposed an amendment making same-sex marriage unconstitutional in both 2004 and 2006 — on neither occasion could it gain the 60 votes needed to overcome a Senate filibuster. Pressure groups are

Examiner tip

Try to get the fractions for the different phases of the amendment process correct. This reassures the examiner that you know what you are doing, and they are easy marks if the amendment process is asked about.

Knowledge check 5

What was 'prohibition'?

keen to press representatives and senators to introduce amendments, as they have the dual benefits of raising the profile of the issue and, because of the importance and emotional pull of the constitution, of motivating supporters.

Debate

The process for amending the constitution is deliberately designed to be difficult, to protect the principles of the system of government set out by the framers. The process does not make amendment impossible, but reflects the federalists' belief that the popular passions need filtering; consequently, a broad and sustained consensus is needed to effect a change. The approval by Congress and the relatively rapid ratification by the states of the 18th Amendment imposing prohibition, and its repeal within 14 years, could suggest that the process is not immune to temporary waves of popular sentiment, and that the requirements of the process are, if anything, not demanding enough.

On the other hand, it would be equally possible to argue that prohibition is the unique exception in 200+ years, and that the framers made a misjudgement in creating such a demanding process. It makes the addition of even widely supported amendments almost impossible, as seen with the failure of the Equal Rights Amendment, despite its approval by the House by 354 votes to 24 and the Senate 84–8, and its ratification by 35 states. The constitution can become 'fossilised': parts which have become obsolete, like the 3rd Amendment, survive, while, more importantly, rights and values which may no longer have majority support are sustained. (It might be pointed out, however, that the 2nd Amendment is *not* currently guilty in this regard, as, according to the most recent Gallup Poll, support for stricter laws on gun sales and possession is at well below 50%). The difficulty of passing constitutional amendments has the effect that the principal means of amending the constitution is through the Supreme Court's power of judicial review, and it is arguable how far this is desirable or democratic.

A further related argument is that the formal process of amendment is not of fundamental significance anyway, since the constitution is sufficiently vague to allow for considerable interpretation and discretion in its implementation. Significant changes have occurred within the system of government without any constitutional change:

- Judicial review is itself not mentioned in the constitution and neither is the federal bureaucracy.
- The 'necessary and proper' clause has allowed Congress to expand its power at the expense of the states.
- The president's power has expanded at the expense of Congress through the 'inherent' powers to be found in such phrases as 'the executive power is vested in the president.'

Evolution of federalism

The relationship between the federal and state governments has been a constant source of political debate in America since the founding of the republic. It goes to the heart of competing visions of America: either one unified nation state with a marked degree of centralised political control, or a confederation of states retaining a considerable degree of autonomy. Stereotypically, those on the left tend to favour a stronger federal government, both to manage the economy and stem the excesses of corporate power, and to ensure basic standards of rights and services. In contrast, those on the right see states as retaining a vital role: they were the foundation of the republic, embody the American ethos of rugged individualism and act as a necessary safeguard against the liberal agenda of the institutions of the federal government.

Federalism in the constitution

'Federalism' is usually defined as a system of government consisting of two more or less autonomous layers with their powers entrenched in a constitution. The term itself does not appear in the constitution drawn up in 1787, and indeed it is arguable how far the system it creates corresponds to this usual definition. The constitution is not explicit on the relationship between the federal and state governments; Article 1, section 8 gives Congress the power to regulate 'commerce among the several states', and section 10 forbids the states from making treaties with other countries, imposing import or export taxes, and maintaining an army. Beyond that, the relationship is implied, and even the 10th Amendment, passed 4 years later, is a negative statement; it does not attempt to delineate what the powers of the states *are*, but rather asserts that they are everything that the federal government is not. It is difficult to claim, therefore, that the powers of the states are entrenched in the constitution, since it does not allocate any explicitly to them; and despite the quite close detail in the enumeration of the powers of Congress, there is, perhaps deliberately, sufficient vagueness to doubt that its powers are entrenched, if that term means they cannot be altered without an amendment to the constitution.

Examiner tip
More than any other topic, federalism seems to encourage candidates to embark on a narrative account, and many answers consist of detailed descriptions of its different phases. Try to focus sharply on the demands of the question in front of you.

The history of federal–state relations has been, from the earliest years, one of steady expansion of the reach of the federal government and the diminution of that of the states. Not only did the powers of the federal government steadily increase, but, from the end of the nineteenth century, the states became increasingly dependent on the federal government through the system of federal grants, a dependence accelerated by the 16th Amendment authorising a federal income tax.

Federalism and the Supreme Court

The Supreme Court has played a crucial role in sanctioning the expansion of the federal government's power, albeit at times reluctantly. A significant decision came as early as 1819 in *McCulloch* v *Maryland*, when the court ruled that the 'necessary and proper' clause (although it was not referred to as such) implied the granting to Congress of such powers as were necessary to implement the powers that *were* explicitly granted. In the particular case, the constitution did not give Congress the power to establish a bank, but the court decided that a bank is an appropriate means of facilitating Congress's power of taxation and spending and, further, that the 'supremacy clause' of Article 6 means that no state has the right to interfere with its operation.

In the twentieth century, the court initially resisted the expansion of congressional power through the New Deal and, in a series of cases, struck down programmes such as the Agriculture Adjustment Act *United States* v *Butler* (1936). However, it eventually gave way in a further series of cases, beginning with *West Coast Hotel* v *Parrish,* decided in 1937. Having conceded the right of Congress to manage the national economy and to impose such measures as it saw fit on the states, the court then took the lead itself after the Second World War in limiting the right of the states to regulate the civil liberties of their own citizens, most famously in *Brown* v *Board of Education of Topeka* (1954).

The New Deal programmes of the 1930s, and the 'war on poverty' and the Great Society programme of the mid-1960s, saw a further expansion of the reach of the federal government. By the 1960s, its role had come to be seen in a positive light; in the minds of many, the state governments had become associated, principally through their attempted frustration of moves to end segregation, with backwardness and repression, and the federal government now represented a positive force, ensuring all citizens had acceptable standards of basic rights and services.

Knowledge check 8

What was the Great Society programme?

However, this perception quickly changed. From the late 1960s onwards many, especially on the right, came to believe that the expansion of the federal role had gone too far. It had shown itself unable to deal with, or was even part responsible for, the social problems of the late 1960s. Increasing drug use and crime, changing sexual morals, and often violent student and racial unrest, meant for many Americans that society seemed on the point of collapse. 'States' rights' became a conservative cause; the federal government had become too powerful and intrusive, presided over by an out-of-touch and profligate Congress, its programmes implemented by an unwieldy and inefficient bureaucracy, imposing its liberal agenda on the rest of the nation. Suspicion of the malign intent of the federal government became ubiquitous in popular culture, and was still evident in later decades in television programmes such as the *X Files.* It manifested itself much more seriously in the bombing of the Alfred P. Murrah Federal Building in Oklahoma City in 1995.

New Federalism

New Federalism was the political expression of this reaction. Beginning under President Nixon, it was an attempt to reverse the flow of power from the states to Washington, and return the balance between the two to that implied in the constitution. The two presidents most associated with New Federalism are Presidents Nixon and Reagan, although the records of both in reducing federal power are decidedly mixed. For example, President Nixon gave (incongruously for a Republican from today's perspective) a high priority to environmental issues; he established the Environmental Protection Agency in 1970, signed amendments to the Clean Air Act into law establishing national air quality standards, and, in response to the oil embargo of 1974, imposed a national speed limit of 55 mph.

By the time of the Reagan presidency, in the aftermath of Watergate and against a background of failed economic policy which had seen a prolonged period of 'stagflation', faith in the federal government had fallen even lower. The president signalled his commitment to the federalist cause when he declared in his inaugural address in 1981 that 'the federal government did not create the states, the states created the federal government'. He was not so much a supporter of the states as keen to reduce government activity at all levels, but even President Reagan was consistently willing to promote new federal regulation when it fitted his policy objectives; for example, the preference of business for national uniform regulation led to the creation of federal trucking standards in 1982.

The high point

The 1990s represented the high point of the New Federalism movement, for a number of reasons:

- The economic growth of the 1990s led to an increase in state revenues, supplemented by the huge influx of funds from the tobacco settlements of the late 1990s, through which major cigarette manufacturers agreed to pay the states a total of $246 billion over 25 years.
- There was an increased willingness by the states to use new methods to solve social problems, particularly related to crime: boot camps were introduced in 27 states; the first 'Megan's Law' was introduced in New Jersey in 1994, followed by federal legislation in 1995; 'three strikes' laws were introduced first in Washington in 1993; New York city pioneered 'zero tolerance'.
- Supreme Court decisions by the so-called 'federalist five' (Justices Rehnquist, O'Connor, Kennedy, Thomas and Scalia), most notably *US* v *Lopez* which, in striking down the Gun-Free School Zones Act of 1990, was the first decision since the New Deal to limit Congress's power under the 'interstate commerce' clause.

Knowledge check 9

What was the intent of the Gun-Free School Zones Act?

The decline

President Bush's rhetoric, both as governor of Texas and at the beginning of his administration, led many to expect that he would adopt a traditionally conservative 'states' rights' approach to the federal–state relationship. However, the overall record of his administration was a disappointment to conservatives; there was no concerted move to shift power back to the states, federal spending rose by about a third through the course of his administration, and he showed himself willing to use the power of the federal government to implement his favoured policy options.

In defence of the president, it could be argued that two of the most often cited examples of federal government expansion his administration oversaw — the creation of the Department of Homeland Security, and the bank bailout legislation of autumn 2008 — were driven by calamitous national events which demanded action from the federal government. However, several programmes could not be justified on these grounds, in particular:

- The 'No Child Left Behind' education legislation passed in 2001 created federal requirements over school syllabus content, testing and teacher qualifications when, as recently as 1996, the Republican Party platform called for the abolition of the federal department of education.
- The Medicare prescription drug benefit, passed in 2003, was widely described as the biggest expansion of the federal role in healthcare since the creation of Medicare itself.

The area of medical ethics saw some of the stranger federal interventions, as the administration and Republican Congress sought to ensure their 'pro-life' values were upheld by the states. In the case of Terri Schiavo, Congress passed legislation transferring jurisdiction just for her case from the state to federal courts, which the president flew to Washington to sign from his holiday in Texas in the early hours of the morning.

Unlike his predecessor, President Obama had never served as a state governor and, as a senator with a voting record that tended liberal, there was no expectation he would emerge as a champion of the states. The Obama healthcare reforms generated heated debate over the constitutional extent of the federal government's powers, and a number of state governments pursued their case through the courts, on the basis that the new federal requirement that every citizen buy health insurance could not be justified by the 'interstate commerce' clause. They enjoyed some initial success, and the Eleventh Circuit Court of Appeals ruled in their favour in August 2011, writing that the new requirement was 'breathtaking in its expansive scope'.

In other areas, the Obama administration encroached on states' autonomy. To the puzzlement of some, but perhaps in an effort to bolster its appeal to 'independent' voters, in 2011 the administration reversed its earlier more emollient approach to the enforcement of federal laws on marijuana. It signalled a similarly robust attitude when it began legal action in a federal court to force the repeal of a new Arizona law, which gave state police new powers over the questioning of suspected illegal immigrants.

Verdict on New Federalism

New Federalism represented a reassertion of the role of the states, and they continue to play a significant role in the life of the nation. Even under an administration as unsympathetic as that of George W. Bush's, they showed a considerable degree of independence. A system of almost universal healthcare was begun in Massachusetts, and same-sex marriage was legalised in a number of states. Several states made public money available for stem cell research, at a time when federal research had been restricted by executive order; in California, Proposition 71 authorised the provision of $3 billion over 10 years. The Global Warming Solutions Act, passed by the California legislature in 2006, sought to cut greenhouse emissions by 25% by 2020, and Governor Schwarzenegger signed a statement of intent with the British prime minister, Tony Blair, to explore solutions to global warming.

However, it would be difficult to argue that New Federalism brought about any fundamental shift in the federal–state relationship, and the experience from 2000 showed its limitations. These limitations were particularly exposed in the economic slowdown from 2008, which put severe pressure on many state budgets, reducing the scope for state initiative. A few states such as Wyoming and North Dakota, with small populations and rising revenues from energy production, were immune, but the majority saw declining revenues and increasing demand for services. Nearly all states are required by their own laws or constitution to run a balanced budget, which means they are much less able to run prolonged deficits than the federal government, and consequently are vulnerable should revenue drop in an economic downturn.

Knowledge check 10

What were the circumstances of the Terri Schiavo case? How did it end?

Examiner tip

In every area of the unit, recent examples are the best evidence to support the points you make. Conflicts between the federal and state governments are frequently reported in the press, so make sure you keep a note of up-to-date and relevant examples.

It is arguable that the role of the federal government *cannot* be significantly rolled back. The operation of a modern society creates a need for centralised management of the economy and for an educated workforce; and the demand for a basic standard of healthcare requires national standards enforced by the federal government. Most significantly perhaps, Congress and the president, whatever their ideological stance, want to exercise control over domestic policy. All presidents have policy goals they wish to achieve, and they are unlikely to willingly renounce the means of achieving them. Similarly, members of Congress are keen to retain control over federal funding of state and district projects, as these are crucial to their prospects of re-election.

Assessment of the constitution

The constitution has been criticised from both sides of the ideological spectrum.

Liberal criticisms

Liberal critics from the early twentieth century onwards have seen the constitution as representing the interests of property and capital. In their view, the desire of the federalists to filter popular opinion, and to separate the different branches of the system, created a system which protects the status quo, and where change of any significance is difficult to bring about. The fragmented government and multiple blocking points frequently lead to gridlock, and the difficulty of amending the constitution has handed an effective veto over many areas of policy to an unelected court. There is an inherent lack of accountability in the system, and power is distributed so broadly that responsibility for any given policy decision is easy to evade. The system allows the erosion of civil liberties during periods of emergency, and the courts have shown themselves slow and unwilling to intervene.

Conservative criticisms

Conservatives' criticisms have focused not so much on the constitution itself but rather on what they would see as the dilution of its principles. In particular, the federal government has exploited the vagueness of the constitution to bring about a vast expansion of its power at the expense of the states, representing a threat to the legitimate rights and interests of property owners and businesses. The illicit growth of the power of the courts through the power of judicial review has led to their imposing their liberal agenda on school prayer, abortion, flag burning and gay rights on the entire country. A specific criticism is that lack of term limits in Congress has been the means of the creation of an unrepresentative political class, devoted only to furthering its own interests.

A non-partisan assessment

The middle-ground defence would first point out that the American Constitution is the longest surviving example in the world. The fact that it is assailed from both left and right suggests that it has somewhere near the right balance between effective government and protection of individual liberty. It has provided political stability and has not prevented change occurring, but rather makes it dependent on broad-based enduring support. It is anyway arguable that lack of change reflects the overall preferences of the American people.

Examiner tip

In any essay answer, do not just describe the arguments of both sides — for example, the different views of conservatives and liberals on the constitution — but *assess* them and make it clear which side you believe is the stronger.

Summary

- The two crucial historical influences on the drawing up of the constitution were the period of arbitrary British rule leading to the revolution, and the dominance of the state legislatures in the years which followed. The first created a suspicion of strong executive power, the second a suspicion of the ambitions of legislatures.
- The structure of the constitution is based around the separation of powers. The first Article is devoted to the legislature, as the representative body of the people; the second to the executive; and the third to the judiciary, the 'least dangerous branch'.
- The principles of the constitution are not stated explicitly, but it embodies the principles of republicanism, checks and balances, separation of powers, federalism and the preservation of individual rights.
- The formal amendment of the constitution is a demanding and only occasionally completed process, but the consistution can effectively be amended through the decisions of the Supreme Court, and executive and legislative action.
- The constitution has been criticised from both left and right, but its endurance over two centuries suggests the framers got it largely right.

Congress

The key issues addressed in this section are:
- the development of Congress's power
- the powers of Congress
- the composition of Congress
- the status of the two chambers
- the relationship between the two chambers
- congressional committees
- the legislative process
- oversight
- power within Congress
- foreign policy
- 'Washington is broken' — is Congress working?

Development of the role of Congress

The experience of the power of the state legislatures in the post-revolutionary period led the framers to impose restrictions on the power of the national legislature, fearing it would go the same way. Consequently, Congress's powers in Article 1, section 8 are closely detailed. These restrictions on the national legislature were reinforced by the 10th Amendment's declaration that all powers not explicitly allocated to Congress were 'reserved to the states'. Yet, whether by design or not, there was still sufficient vagueness in Article 1 to allow for the expansion of Congress's power far beyond the apparently narrow constraints of section 8:
- The power to provide for the 'general welfare' has provided the justification for federal social programmes.
- The 'interstate commerce' clause has provided the justification for expansion of federal regulation, including, for example, the Civil Rights Act.

- The 'necessary and proper' clause has provided the basis for an increased role in a range of other areas of national life.
- The 'supremacy' clause in Article 6 explicitly makes congressional laws superior to state law in the areas in which it has jurisdiction.

Bipartisan Campaign Reform Act The BCRA was the most significant congressional attempt at campaign finance reform in 30 years. It banned the receipt and expenditure of 'soft money' by national political parties and placed limits on the broadcasting of so-called 'issue ads'.

Congress's power has grown to the extent that Congress is often spoken of as among the most powerful legislatures in the world. The separation of powers ensures that, unlike many legislatures, including that of the UK, Congress is not the creature of the executive. Many laws are initiated by members of Congress, such as the McCain-Feingold Bipartisan Campaign Reform Act passed in 2002, and the president has few formal means of controlling Congress. Even a Congress controlled by the president's party may reject his proposals, and he often needs to rely on his powers of persuasion to get anything done. Congress scrutinises the executive through the confirmation of appointments and the oversight of executive departments, and it has the sole power of the purse to control both the budget and the allocation of finances. It can reject the president's budget partially or even wholly; recently, for example, Congress thwarted a key pledge of the Obama administration, the closure of the Guantanamo Bay detention centre, through the passage of legislation barring the use of federal funds to transfer detainees from Guantanamo to the USA.

However, there are also distinct limits to Congress's power. Congress is not sovereign in the same sense as the UK Parliament, and its laws may be struck down by the Supreme Court. Some congressional powers have been effectively taken over by the president, for example the power to declare war, and significant areas still remain the responsibility of the states. Congress was envisaged by the constitution as the most significant branch of government but, as the need for national leadership arose, it was inevitable that a Congress comprised of 535 individuals and two equal houses with different constituencies would cede its agenda-setting role to the president, the only nationally elected figure. Congressmen and senators are preoccupied with re-election and meeting local concerns, which hampers their ability to take a national view; a frequent criticism is that local interests are over-represented at the expense of the national interest.

Powers of Congress

The powers explicitly allocated to Congress are laid out in Article 1; some are shared between the houses, and some are exclusive to one house.

Shared powers

The powers shared by the House of Representatives and the Senate are as follows:
- To pass legislation, and all powers of tax raising and spending; both houses have equal power, and all bills pass all stages in both houses; both have full power of detailed scrutiny and amendment ✓
- To conduct investigations of the executive branch
- To initiate constitutional amendments
- To declare war
- To approve appointment of the vice-president if a vacancy should arise

Exclusive powers

The exclusive powers of the House of Representatives reflect this body's original role as the voice of the people. These powers are as follows:
- To begin consideration of all revenue-raising bills
- To bring impeachment charges against any member of the executive or judicial branch on a simple majority
- To elect the president if no candidate has an overall majority in the Electoral College

The Senate's exclusive powers reflect the original role of this house as a deliberative body. These powers are as follows:
- To ratify all treaties negotiated by the president, two-thirds majority required
- To try cases of impeachment, two-thirds majority required to convict and remove office holders
- To confirm nominations to the executive and judicial branches by the president, a simple majority required
- To elect the vice-president if there is no overall majority in the Electoral College

Composition of Congress

House of Representatives

The House of Representatives consists of 435 members, each representing a district (the US equivalent of a UK constituency). House representatives are sometimes referred to as 'congressmen' and congresswomen', but these terms are not used of senators. States are allocated districts on the basis of their population (the least populous states such as Wyoming have just one representative), with the allocation being changed every 10 years to reflect population shifts between states. The states are themselves responsible for the division of the state into congressional districts, and the addition or subtraction of districts from the state's allocation requires redistricting.

Senate

The Senate consists of 100 members. Each state is allocated two senators irrespective of population, which means that states with small populations are disproportionately represented. (Wyoming, for example, has more representation in the Senate than in the House.) Defenders of Senate representation claim that equal representation is an important element of the federal nature of the constitution, but it does mean that the interests of the rural population, for example agriculture, guns and energy production, are given disproportionate influence, at the expense of the majority living in the cities.

Status of the two chambers

The Senate is usually considered to have greater prestige than the House. Senators are fewer in number and enjoy a longer tenure. The exclusive powers of the Senate are usually seen as more significant, and almost every presidential election field has at least one senator as a live candidate, but rarely a House representative.

Examiner tip

Examination candidates often believe that the House of Representatives has the 'sole power of the purse', when in fact it only has the power to begin hearing revenue-raising bills. Make sure you are clear about this.

Redistricting The redrawing of district boundaries; in most states this is carried out by the state legislatures, although a minority use an independent commission. Where the process is under political control, frequently the majority party will attempt to gain some party advantage through gerrymandering the districts.

Knowledge check 11

Which state gained most districts through the reallocation of districts based on the 2010 census?

Knowledge check 12

What is the origin and meaning of the term 'gerrymander'?

Consequently, senators are seen by most as more influential and enjoying greater prestige; House members will often aspire to join the Senate but movement in the other direction is almost unknown. However, there is no single senator with the same status and profile as the House Speaker who, when the White House is in the hands of the opposite party, assumes the role of national leader of the opposition, as Nancy Pelosi did in the last 2 years of the Bush presidency, and John Boehner has (to some extent) under President Obama.

Consequences of differences in size and area represented

House of Representatives

- House representatives are specialists: they serve on one or two standing committees and their areas of specialism are often linked to the concerns of their district.
- House representatives have fewer constituents than almost all senators (far fewer in some cases), so there is a closer relationship between them. As they are elected every 2 years, House members tend to be highly responsive to the views of their constituents.
- The size of the House means its organisation needs to be more bureaucratic, with the Speaker in overall control, and with strict rules on debate on the floor of the chamber.

Senate

- Senators are generalists: they usually serve on two or three standing committees, and are more concerned than House representatives with national and international issues.
- Senators represent a broader range of opinion than most House members. As they are elected for a 6-year term, they need not be as immediately responsive to constituents' views.
- The Senate is traditionally more collegiate and consensual. There is no equivalent of the Speaker (the vice-president is president of the Senate but only takes the chair if a vote is tied), and it is less committee-based and less needful of rules, for example there is no limit on debate. It is more resistant to centralised leadership, and the power of the filibuster symbolises its individual nature.

The changing Senate

A number of factors have combined to change the traditional image of the Senate as an exclusive non-partisan club, detached from the raw politics of the House of Representatives. The rapidly increasing costs of Senate elections (the average winning candidate spent $7.5 million in 2008, compared to $3.7 million in 1996) mean that, even with 6 years between elections, senators now have to spend as much time as possible in their states, fundraising for the next one. Most Senate votes are consequently scheduled between Tuesday and Thursday, and with senators spending most of the week outside Washington, traditional social bonds are weaker. A higher proportion of the Senate is now made up of former House representatives — for example, half of the 2008–10 senators had previously served in the House, whereas, 30 years before, fewer than a third had — and they bring the more combative ethos of the House with them. In contrast, former governors, who tend to be less partisan, are now much fewer in number. Aides have proliferated in recent years and are often more ideological than the senators they serve, pushing them to take more entrenched positions.

Relationship between the two chambers

The balance of power between the two houses can lie with either, dependent on the dynamic of the time.

When the president is attempting to push measures through a Congress controlled by his own party, the Senate often has a greater influence on the shape of the final legislation. This is because:

- as they represent a whole state rather than a district, senators tend to be more moderate, and, as only a third are elected at any one time, there is rarely a strong sense of mandate behind the president's proposals, or a sense that they owe their election to him
- the increasingly routine use of the filibuster means a 'supermajority' of 60 is always required for even faintly controversial legislation

In contrast, the House tends to be more partisan and, since all its members are elected simultaneously, can exhibit a strong sense of mandate. The frustrations House members sometimes feel with the slower pace and more centrist outlook of the Senate were expressed by Sam Rayburn, a Texas Democrat, who was House Speaker in the 1940s and 1950s and was famously quoted as saying: 'The Republicans are the opposition. The Senate is the enemy.'

Greater Senate influence was evident on a number of occasions during President Obama's first 2 years. The final healthcare legislation was based on the Senate version, which the House was forced to pass as it stood. The climate-change bill, which passed the House, subsequently died in the Senate. Press reports characterised House Democrats as 'expendable shock troops, able to move quickly and put pressure on the Senate to strike a deal'. The same pattern was observable during the period of the Bush administration when the Republicans controlled both houses. Ray LaHood, then a Republican representative remarked, 'There's no question the president is tilted toward what the Senate wants and tilted against what the House has done. We do all the heavy lifting and fall on our swords [even] when it's not going to be the final product.'

However, if Congress (or just the House) is controlled by the opposing party to the president, the House will often take the lead in opposing him, and may attempt to move its own agenda forward. Given the right circumstances, the House can exercise considerable influence. This was apparent in the negotiations over the raising of

Knowledge check 14

What office did President Obama appoint Ray LaHood to?

What was the Contract with America?

the debt limit in July and August 2011, when conservatives in the House Republican conference effectively set the terms of the final deal. There are, however, distinct constitutional limits on what the House can achieve single-handedly, as was apparent by the failure of most the items in the 1994 Contract with America.

The filibuster

The **filibuster**, contrary to what many examinees believe, is not to be found anywhere in the constitution but was adopted as procedure by the Senate in 1806. Prior to this, debate could be ended through a simple majority vote but, thereafter, senators were able to speak for as long as they wished to. In the twentieth century, the power of the filibuster was attenuated, with the adoption of a rule that debate could be ended through a two-thirds majority vote, later reduced to 60. What is not always appreciated is that modern-day filibusters do not consist of any individual senator actually talking for any length of time at all. Through a procedure adopted in 1975, with the intention of keeping the floor of the chamber clear for other business, all that is needed is the announcement of a *threat* to filibuster for a 60-vote majority to be required to pass the threatened legislation.

Congressional committees

Composition

The party balance in all committees is in the same proportion as the chamber as a whole. Committee chairs are always drawn from the majority party, and traditionally are appointed according to the seniority rule (that the chair is the member of majority party with longest continuous service on that committee) although this is not always followed now. Membership of a committee is a key opportunity to exercise influence, especially over home district interests, and so is keenly sought.

Functions of different committees

- **Standing committees** are permanent policy-specialist committees, 17 in each house, and combine legislative and scrutiny functions. They conduct the committee stage of the legislative process and carry out investigations within their policy area. In the Senate, they begin the confirmation process of the numerous presidential appointments.
- **The House Rules Committee** timetables bills in the House, moving bills from the committee stage to the second reading. It assigns priorities to bills and gives a 'rule' to each bill passing onto the floor for its second reading, setting out the rules of debate, for example whether amendments are permitted from the floor. It is a key tool of political control of the House.
- **Conference committees** have an ad hoc membership drawn from both houses. They have just one function — the reconciliation of different versions of the same bill which emerge from the two houses. Conference committees can be a focus of political tension when the two houses are under different political control, as they were from 2001–03, and when the Republicans took over the House in 2011.

- **Select committees** also have an ad hoc membership. They are set up either when an investigation does not fall within the policy area of one standing committee, or is likely to be very time-consuming.

The legislative process

There are seven stages to the legislative process:

- **Introduction/first reading:** This is the formal introduction of a bill. There is no debate or vote. A significant proportion of legislation is presidential initiative, and will be introduced by the highest-ranking member of the president's own party on the relevant committee.
- **Committee stage:** First, the Speaker decides which committee to assign a particular bill to, and the committee chair then assigns it in turn to a sub-committee. The standing committees have full power of amendment; the sub-committees will hold hearings with witnesses (who are chosen by the sub-committee chair, often to support their own position) and carry out line-by-line consideration ('mark-up') of the bill. The amended bill then returns to the whole committee for further consideration (committee members tend to defer to the judgement of the sub-committee), after which it goes back to the floor of the chamber (it is 'reported out').
- **Timetabling:** In the House, the House Rules Committee decides the legislative priorities of bills waiting to come to the floor and the rules for debate.
- **Floor debate/second reading:** This is the first opportunity for most members to debate the bill. Passage of the bill requires a simple majority, although increasingly in the Senate a majority of 60 is needed.
- **Conference committee:** This stage is required to reconcile differences between House and Senate versions of the same bill. Not all bills will go through a formal conference committee; in the case of the healthcare legislation passed in 2010, for example, the House was forced to abandon its own version and adopt the Senate's version.
- **Final approval:** Both houses are required to approve the conference version; no amendment is possible, only approval or rejection.
- **Presidential approval:** The president has to approve legislation before it finally becomes a law. The president can either approve or veto legislation. If he chooses to veto, the bill is sent back to Congress with an explanation, and Congress then has the option of either abandoning it or overriding the veto with a two-thirds vote in both houses. If the president chooses to approve, and it is legislation he is keen to identify himself with, there will be an elaborate public signing ceremony. If the president is less keen to identify himself with the legislation, the signing is carried out behind closed doors.

Examiner tip

Try to get the different majorities required by different congressional procedures right. Many students believe, for example, that a two-thirds majority is required to pass legislation, when in fact it is a simple majority.

Knowledge check 16

What was the last presidential veto overridden by Congress?

Assessment

Although only the president has the formal power of veto, at each of the seven stages there is the potential to block a bill. This is an important part of the explanation as to why so few bills are ultimately passed.

The positive view of this complex legislative process is that it means the passage of legislation entails detailed scrutiny by experts, and requires a broad and sustained consensus, compromise and usually bipartisan support. Consequently, legislation will be thoroughly examined and should represent the most accurate reflection of the nation's collective wishes. This contrasts favourably with the UK government's control of Parliament, where legislation can be pushed through the House of Commons with token scrutiny and the support of a quiescent majority based, in the case of the Labour government of 2005–10 for example, on 35% of the vote.

The negative view is that the multiple blocking points means legislation can be halted by a few key individuals, especially committee chairs, who may be acting for any number of motives unconnected with the greater good of the public. In particular, it may allow wealthy campaign donors to exercise disproportionate influence through the obstruction of politicians they sponsor, which contributes to wider public cynicism about the role of money in Congress. The increasingly routine use of the filibuster in the Senate means that 41 senators, representing less than a quarter of the population, can block what many might see as important legislation. Fundamentally, it is a system strongly biased in favour of the status quo; significant change may be difficult or impossible to bring about, or emerge in a final form so diluted as to be ineffectual.

Oversight

'Oversight' is the general term for Congress's monitoring of the activity of federal departments and agencies, and its scrutiny of presidential nominations and treaties by the Senate. Oversight is exercised through the standing committees, the select committees as and when they are created, and also through the Government Accountability Office (GAO).

Government Accountability Office (GAO) The GAO is an independent agency that works for Congress. Its work is not unlike that of the National Audit Office in the UK; it investigates whether federal funds are being spent efficiently, and reports on how well government programmes and policies are meeting their objectives.

There are a number of factors which should, in theory, make oversight more effective than in a parliamentary system such as the UK's. Traditionally, US party discipline is weak, and congressional careers are based around the permanent standing committees rather than promotion to the executive. However, although there have been high-profile exceptions, such as the investigations into Watergate and Iran Contra (both some time ago), the reality is that oversight is not always effectively carried out. In particular, when the presidency and Congress are controlled by the same party, partisan loyalties have been seen to undermine oversight. It was noticeable, for example, that during joint Republican control from 2002–06, on a variety of indicators, such as hearings held and reports issued, oversight declined. Then, on the resumption of Democratic control in 2007, there was an immediate increase in the level of oversight.

The motivation of members of Congress is also a factor. Like all politicians, members of Congress are driven in large part by a desire to be re-elected, and oversight offers them little by way of benefits either to themselves or their constituents. Nor does it improve their chances of re-election. Some members will seek to make a name for themselves as zealous pursuers of executive incompetence but they are relatively few in number.

Appointment

The vast majority of presidential appointments are uncontroversial, except for those to the judiciary. The process of confirmation by the Senate has been criticised because very few nominees are rejected, and there is a long history of the confirmation of administration officials who later prove to be incompetent. A recent high-profile example was Michael Brown, head of FEMA at the time of Hurricane Katrina.

Treaties

The majority of treaties are approved by the Senate; when they are not, personal and/or partisan hostility rather than objective analysis can often be discerned as the principal motivation. Cabot's hostility to the president was behind the rejection of the League of Nations Treaty in 1919, and resentment over the failed impeachment and 'Clinton's War' in Kosovo behind the rejection of the Comprehensive Test Ban Treaty in 1999. The New START Treaty was ratified in December 2010 but, despite the existence of a considerable consensus over its merits (it was supported by the joint chiefs of staff and at least six former Republican secretaries of state), the desire not to give the president a political victory was a more powerful motivation for most Republican senators; it was ultimately ratified 71–26, with fewer than a third of Republicans voting to support it.

Power within Congress

There are two potential sources of power and leadership in Congress, the party leaderships and the standing committee chairmen.

The constitution predisposes to party weakness. The separation of executive and legislature means that party loyalties are weaker than in a parliamentary system. This is because legislators are not elected as potential supporters or members of the executive, but rather to represent the interests of their districts or states and to wrest as much federal bounty out of the system for them as possible. Whereas in a parliamentary system, party loyalty can be bought through the prospect of a job in the executive, Congress has its own career structure — the position of committee chair has traditionally been, and to some extent still is, dependent on seniority, not party patronage. Members of Congress are elected through campaigns fought largely with resources they have generated themselves; campaigns are candidate-centred, and many congressional campaign ads will not mention the name of the candidate's party at all. Candidates are not dependent on their party for either finance or organisation; they are often more dependent on interest groups, whose assistance creates a source of competing loyalty.

Party leadership

The **Speaker** of the House of Representatives is the single most high-profile politician in Congress. He or she acts as presiding officer of the chamber, is responsible for the planning and implementation of the legislative agenda, and has the power to decide which committee to refer bills to.

The Speaker is elected by the entire membership of the House of Representatives and was not traditionally a partisan figure. However, effectively, the Speaker is

Knowledge check 17

What is FEMA?

Knowledge check 18

On what charges was President Clinton impeached?

the nominee of the majority party, and, as the parties polarised from the 1980s onwards, increasingly the Speaker's role became to promote their party's agenda, particularly when the White House was controlled by the opposing party.

Different Speakers have different styles. Dennis Hastert, who was Speaker from 1999 to 2007, operated very much behind the scenes, while the House majority leader Tom DeLay ('the Hammer') drove the Republican agenda through the House. His successor, Nancy Pelosi, partly at least because for the first 2 years she was countering a Republican president, sought a much higher public profile as an opposition leader to the president, and delivered as many floor speeches in first 16 months of her tenure as Hastert delivered in 8 years.

Standing committee chairs

Standing committee chairs have traditionally been able to run their committees with more or less complete autonomy. They have the power to:

- 'pigeonhole' bills, delaying their consideration indefinitely
- control the committee's agenda, i.e. the order in which bills are discussed
- determine the timing and frequency of meetings and public hearings
- exert significant influence over the number and composition of sub-committees, and the selection of sub-committee chairs

The chairmanship of a standing committee is the pinnacle of a congressional career for many members of Congress, and can bring considerable benefits for the district or state they represent. Loss of a congressional chair through a change in political control of Congress is usually greeted with much lamenting in the local press.

Pigeonhole A committee chair can 'pigeonhole' a bill, which means that the bill is put to one side and its progress terminated.

Party revival

Despite the factors working against them, from the 1980s onwards the party leaders became more powerful, in the House particularly. Confronted by the ideological administration of Ronald Reagan, Democrats were willing to strengthen party leaders, and the House Speaker Tip O'Neill in particular had the role of formulating a Democratic alternative to Reagan's programme.

This process of accumulation of power by the party leaderships advanced further through the Speakership of Newt Gingrich from 1995 to 1998. Gingrich, through the national manifesto of the Contract with America, attempted to reclaim the role as national agenda-setter for Congress, and the Republican leadership in particular, from the president. Such was the momentum behind Speaker Gingrich and the House Republicans that President Clinton was famously forced to declare in March 1995 that 'the constitution gives me relevance'; his position was only revived by the Oklahoma City bombing the following month, which enabled him to command the national stage in the role of spokesman for the nation.

Gingrich was succeeded as Speaker after the unexpected Republican losses in the 1998 midterms by Dennis Hastert, who was succeeded himself by Nancy Pelosi in

January 2007 on the Democratic takeover of Congress. John Boehner became Speaker in January 2011 after the Republicans regained control of the House. All three have to a greater or lesser extent maintained the Gingrich model of tight party control. The methods they have employed include:

- ignoring seniority in assigning committee chairs in favour of favoured party candidates; for example, Nancy Pelosi engineered the replacement of John Dingell by Henry Waxman as House Energy and Commerce Committee chairman
- tight monitoring of the progress of favoured legislation through its various stages, sometimes imposing timetables on committees for completion, and even instructing committees to make little or no revision
- 'leadership' PACs, set up by members of the party leadership to distribute campaign contributions to build a network of dependants
- working with majority members of the Rules Committee to design the rule likely to produce the bill which most closely meets majority party views, for example prohibiting hostile amendments
- exploiting the power of the Speaker to select the membership of conference committees to exclude minority members — Hastert and DeLay were known to make deals and even add major provisions after the conference closed
- increasing use of the practice of earmarking to help vulnerable members — in the 10 years after 1994, when the Republicans took control of Congress, the number of home-district earmarks increased tenfold; the 2005 Transport Bill reportedly contained 6,000+

> **Knowledge check 19**
>
> What is earmarking? What has been its significance in Congress?

The Senate is usually more resistant to centralised partisan leadership for a number of reasons. First, because senators have to represent the views of an entire state, they are usually more centrist. There is no equivalent to the Speaker who can make a play for a national audience, and the much smaller numbers in the Senate means there is less need for rules of procedure and enforcement by a centralised authority. Smaller numbers also mean senators are more open to informal negotiation and compromise. However, the Senate has not been immune to the polarising forces at work since the 1980s and, according to Norman Ornstein, the impeachment trial of President Clinton in 1999 marked a decisive shift: 'Senators now saw themselves as members of their respective political parties first — and representatives of their constituencies second.'

Limits of party control

Although party unity is now at levels unimaginable 35 years ago, the first consideration for any member of Congress is still how their vote will be seen by the electorate at home. If their electoral needs are better served by a vote against their party, party loyalty becomes an expendable commodity. A significant number of Democrats voted against most of the major first-term initiatives of the Obama administration; of the six Democratic senators who voted against the legislation authorising the raising of the US debt ceiling in August 2011, for example, several like Kirsten Gillibrand of New York were facing an election in 2012 and needed to send a signal of solidarity to their party's base, whose support would be crucial in the forthcoming campaign.

> **Knowledge check 20**
>
> How many senators face re-election in any one election?

Foreign policy

The constitution sets out a clear role for Congress in foreign policy, and explicitly allocates a number of foreign policy powers:

- to declare war
- to regulate trade with foreign nations
- to provide for the common defence
- to raise and support armies
- to confirm ambassadors
- to ratify treaties

Knowledge check 21

Congress has only declared war five times since 1787 — when?

The division of responsibility for foreign policy between Congress and the president sets up what has famously been described as 'an invitation to struggle' for its control.

There has been a discernible pattern in the history of this struggle; during a crisis, the nation looks to the president for leadership and direction, so that Congress will tend to defer to him, for example at the height of the Cold War and the immediate period after September 11, 2001. However, at other times, when there is no immediate threat to the nation, Congress will often attempt to assert itself, such as the period of détente in the 1970s or the post-Cold War period of the 1990s, especially if Congress is controlled by the opposing party to the president. During these periods, the House Speaker or other prominent members of the opposition in Congress will challenge the president and may even attempt to run an alternative foreign policy — evident, for example, in the visits of Speakers Dennis Hastert to Columbia in 1999 and Nancy Pelosi to Syria in 2007. The Republican Senate from 1994 onwards, and particularly the Senate Foreign Affairs Committee under the chairmanship of Jesse Helms, was active in passing legislation, such as the Helms Burton Act and the Iraq Liberation Act, at odds with the wishes of the president. More routinely, members of Congress will show a keen interest in managing and adjusting to their own preferences programmes dependent on annual appropriation measures such as foreign aid, where Congress has significant leverage.

Effectiveness of the congressional role

There are a number of factors militating against Congress making an effective contribution to foreign policy.

Disunity

Congress is a disunified body, comprising two equal houses and 535 individuals, all representing disparate interests, and which struggles to speak with one voice. In foreign policy especially, there is a need for clear direction and leadership, which only the executive is able to provide.

Parochialism

Although some senators make foreign relations a speciality, generally members of Congress rarely have any foreign policy experience. Members of Congress, particularly in the House, are focused on re-election and driven by the local interests of constituents and donors, to which international issues are a secondary concern.

When parochial concerns demand a foreign policy expression, they can be at odds with official policy and act to undermine it. For example, twice in recent years, most recently in 2010, the House Foreign Affairs Committee has passed a resolution condemning the deaths of over a million Armenians at the hands of Turkey during the First World War as genocide, despite requests from the administration to refrain for fear of damage to the important strategic relationship with Turkey. It is not a coincidence that significant numbers of the relatively small Armenian-American population are concentrated in the districts of those House members pressing for the resolution's approval.

Congress's performance in its role to regulate foreign trade is a further illustration of the limiting influence of parochialism. The actual negotiation of trade deals has long passed to the president, but Congress retains the power to approve them. The president needs to be able to negotiate trade deals with foreign governments without the prospect of the deal negotiated unravelling in Congress and, to this end, 'fast-track' authority was granted to the president under the Trade Act 1974. The Act expired in 1994 and, although it was renewed for 2002–07, it has not been renewed further, either for President Bush or for President Obama; Congress is too reluctant to give up the power to promote the local interests of constituents and clients to give the president a power which many would view as in the clear national interest.

> **Knowledge check 22**
>
> How does fast-track authority work?

Election preoccupation

Preoccupation with re-election can affect foreign policy in a number of ways. Members of Congress are aware they may suffer electorally if they can be portrayed by rivals as too concerned with international issues, at the expense of their district or state. Preoccupation with electoral calculations makes congressmen risk-averse; any credit for foreign policy successes will go to the president, but support for an unpopular policy may well be exploited by opponents. John Kerry's vote for the invasion of Iraq was a complication for him in the 2004 presidential campaign, and it worked in favour of the then Senator Obama in the 2008 Democratic primaries that he was elected after the Iraq vote in the Senate. In contrast, Hillary Clinton's vote in support of the invasion was a factor undermining her credibility with the Democratic base.

Presidential evasion

There are several ways in which the president is able to circumvent the need to involve Congress in foreign policy decisions:

Power as commander-in-chief

Although only Congress has the power to declare war or authorise any long-term deployment of troops, the president can commit troops in his role as commander-in-chief. Congress is then left to react to his decisions, and will always be reluctant to be seen to undermine troops committed to action, rendering its role peripheral if not meaningless. President Truman despatched forces to Korea in 1950 under the cover of a UN 'police action', with no vote and only informal congressional involvement; President Johnson escalated the US campaign in Vietnam in 1965 on the basis of the Gulf of Tonkin resolution passed the previous year, which merely authorised the president to 'to take all necessary measures' in response to an isolated attack on a

US ship. These two cases, which arguably only continued a pattern of presidential war-making started in the nineteenth century, have set the pattern for subsequent conflicts.

The president can choose to seek congressional authorisation if it suits him, as it gives a stronger mandate and spreads political responsibility; for example, President Bush secured congressional approval through votes in both houses on the campaigns in Afghanistan in 2001 and Iraq in 2002. He can choose the timing of such votes to maximise the chances of a favourable outcome; the vote for action against Iraq was set for October 2002, just before the 2002 midterms, in order to put maximum pressure on any wavering members of Congress engaged in re-election campaigns. However, if a positive vote is not achievable, presidents have shown few qualms about pressing ahead anyway, and the Kosovo campaign in 1999 was the first conflict in American history conducted in face of an explicit refusal by Congress to authorise it.

Knowledge check 23

How did Congress authorise the invasion of Afghanistan in 2001?

The War Powers Act

The increasing resistance to unilateral presidential war-making in the later stages of the Vietnam War led to the passage of the War Powers Act, passed in 1973 over President Nixon's veto.

This reasserted Congress's power over the deployment of troops into conflict: it restated that either specific authorisation or a formal declaration of war by Congress is needed for such deployments, and if the president has to act in an emergency, he is required to obtain congressional approval within 60 days. If this is refused, forces must be withdrawn within 30 days.

However, it has not been seen to be an effective restraint, and can be argued to have had the effect of *increasing* presidential power, as it gave the president the statutory authority for the first time to wage war without congressional declaration, albeit only for 90 days. No president has recognised the constitutionality of the War Powers Act and, at least until Afghanistan and Iraq, presidents have generally sought only short-term engagements with little use of ground forces, as was the case, for example, in Grenada in 1983, Libya in 1986, and Kosovo in 1999.

As significantly, Congress has been seen to lack the political will to enforce the Act's provisions. Legislators are risk-averse, and are reluctant to vote against the president when troops are committed to action. Attempts by individual congressmen to involve the federal courts have not been successful, the courts ruling that they could not be used as a fallback for legislators whose views are not shared by a majority of both houses.

Power of the purse

Given the colossal cost of military operations, the power of the purse is potentially Congress's most effective restraint on the president's use of force but it has not usually proved effective. Despite increasing opposition within Congress to the Vietnam War from the late 1960s onwards, it took until 1973 to cut off funding, after the Paris Peace Accords had been signed, which officially brought hostilities to an end. More recently, the 2007–09 Democratic Congress failed to impose conditions on continued funding for operations in Iraq, although this had been one of the main commitments which the Democratic leadership had campaigned on. In both cases, the president was able to play on Congress's reluctance to be seen to abandon troops in the field, and to make effective use of his veto power. An exception to this general pattern was the success of the Boland Amendments in the 1980s in cutting off funds to the Nicaraguan Contras, forcing elements of the Reagan administration into illegality to evade them.

Conclusion

Despite the shared powers in the constitution, the president has assumed control for the direction and tone of foreign policy, which has proved to be especially firm over military deployment. Recent history suggests that attempts at congressional reassertion, either through the power of the purse or through other means such as the War Powers Act, are likely to be ineffective. Congress may be able to influence some other areas of foreign policy but overall its role has become marginal.

Is Congress working?

'Washington is broken'

At the time of the passage of healthcare legislation in 2010, and again during the negotiations around legislation to raise the debt ceiling in 2011, the inability to produce a solution to obvious and serious problems meant that the accusation was frequently heard that 'Washington is broken'. (A recent academic study of Congress was titled 'The Broken Branch'.)

How sustainable is this charge? There are permanent institutional features of Congress that make decision making difficult. This is the inevitable consequence of a process whereby legislation needs to be approved by two equal chambers, which may be under the control of different parties, as well as the complexity of the legislative procedure within each and the multiple veto points it creates. The separation of powers means that congressmen and senators stand for re-election on their service to their own constituents, and have only a limited incentive to take a broader view of the national interest; members of Congress need not worry unduly that the approval rating of the institution as a whole is under 20% if their own rating with their own constituents is enough to secure re-election. There is a further particular issue with the unrepresentative nature of the Senate, which means that under a quarter of the population elects the 41 senators who have an effective veto over any legislation.

Knowledge check 24

How can 41 senators exercise an effective veto?

Added to these permanent features are a number of recent developments. Trust in Congress has not been enhanced, for example, by the steady stream of salacious revelations concerning members of Congress, but the most significant is the increased partisanship within Congress, which has made partisan wrangling and the deadlock it produces Washington's default condition.

Increased partisanship is the product of a number of factors:
- The parties have become more ideologically distinct since the 1980s, as the Republican Party became more consistently conservative and the Democratic Party more consistently liberal.

- In the House, partisan gerrymandering has led to the creation of safe one-party districts, which has rendered many representatives only vulnerable to a primary challenge. Since primary voters are the party faithful, and are more ideologically motivated than the general population, the challenge will invariably come from the further extremes of the party, and to forestall this Republican representatives have to move to the right and Democratic representatives to the left.
- Ideological interest groups, such as the Club for Growth and Citizens United on the right, and MoveOn.org on the left, actively campaign against representatives and senators not deemed to be sufficiently in sympathy with their values. In the 2010 primaries, long-established senators such as John McCain in Arizona and Blanche Lincoln in Arkansas were challenged by candidates sponsored by such groups.
- The growth of a partisan media, such as Fox News on the right and MSNBC on the left, and the proliferation of the blogosphere, help generate partisan pressure.
- The rising cost of elections and the constant need to fundraise, even for senators with 6-year election cycles, means that less time is spent in Washington, with decreased opportunities for personal relationships with members of Congress from the opposition party to develop. Because party control of Congress has become so keenly contested, parties now require six-figure contributions from members of Congress to go towards campaigning in key districts and states, strengthening the need to fundraise further. In an article in *Time* in 2010, former representative Dan Glickman argued that the need to raise money reduces any incentive for bipartisanship; problems left unsolved can be fundraising boons, since wealthy interests are forced to keep 'working the Hill' if issues are left unresolved, pouring more and more money into campaign coffers.

The consequences of increased partisanship have been as follows:
- An increase in 'party votes' and confrontation between the parties have become the norm. The Obama stimulus package in 2009 and the healthcare legislation which finally passed in 2010 were unanimously opposed by the Republican Party in the House and by nearly the entire party in the Senate at all their stages.
- The use of the filibuster in the Senate has become almost routine, such that a majority of 60 is required for any faintly contentious legislation.
- Congressional procedure has been abused to ensure partisan victories; for example, roll call votes on legislation on the House floor, which usually last 15 minutes, have been extended to 1–3 hours while the hunt goes on for the votes to pass it, and the roll call vote for the passage of Medicare reform in 2003 was reportedly the longest in congressional history.
- The oversight function has become dysfunctional and driven by partisan loyalty.
- A breakdown in civility, epitomised by the shout of 'you lie' at the president during his 2009 address to both houses of Congress.

Knowledge check 25

What is a party vote?

Washington isn't broken

There is plenty of evidence that the case condemning 'Washington' has been overstated. Legislation which can attract broad sustained support *will* pass, for example the Welfare Reform Bill initiated by the Republican leadership and signed by President Clinton in 1996, the No Child Left Behind Bill of 2003, which was the initiative of President Bush and co-sponsored by Ted Kennedy, and the bank bailout bill at the end of the Bush presidency. The 111th Congress in the first 2 years of the

Obama administration was described on Bloomberg as being '...probably the most productive session of Congress since at least the 1960s'; it saw the passage of a major stimulus package, healthcare reform and reform of the financial services industry. The legislation to raise the debt ceiling was passed in August 2011 with truly bipartisan majorities, the 'extremes' in both parties voting against and the centrists in both voting for — the archetypal product of congressional negotiation and compromise.

Party unity has certainly increased but the limits of party control were observable, for example, in the 34 Democratic representatives who voted against the final House version of the healthcare legislation, nearly all of whom were from districts which had voted for John McCain in 2008. This strongly suggests that it is the still the case that, if there is a conflict between party and district loyalties, congressmen will always 'vote the district'.

Finally, some commentators, such as Charles Krauthammer in the *Washington Post*, have argued that a failure of leadership is the root of the problems that have afflicted Congress since 2009. The complaint that America had become 'ungovernable' was heard in the Carter years, also with a Democratic president and Congress, and it arguably illustrates more than anything the need for the president to manage Congress successfully. In the case of the 2010 healthcare legislation, for example, it is arguable that President Obama 'overlearnt' the Clinton experience with his healthcare reforms, which were presented as a fait accompli to Congress and then went nowhere; President Obama consequently handed over too much power to the party leadership in Congress, which led to uncertainty over what he wanted, and made it difficult to rally public support behind the proposals.

Knowledge check 26

Why would representatives from districts which voted for John McCain be minded to oppose President Obama's healthcare reforms?

Summary

- Although the formal powers of Congress are closely defined in Article 1 of the constitution, there has proved nevertheless to be sufficient vagueness for these powers to expand, particularly in the twentieth century.
- Some of the formal powers of Congress are shared between the two houses, for example to pass legislation, and some are exclusive to one, for example the power of the Senate to confirm presidential appointments.
- The House of Representatives is made up of 435 representatives (or congressmen and congresswomen), the number per state decided on the basis of population; and the Senate consists of 100 senators, two per state irrespective of population.
- Traditionally the Senate is seen as the more prestigious chamber, although both houses have the political initiative at different times.
- The most important congressional committees are the standing committees in both houses, which have the role of scrutinising legislation and carrying out oversight of the executive.
- The legislative process is long and its many stages mean there are many opportunities for opponents to block the progress of a bill.
- Oversight of the executive is an important function of Congress but is infrequently carried out effectively.
- Within Congress there are two competing sources of leadership — the committee chairs and the party leadership — and in recent years the party leadership has become more dominant.
- Although the constitution shares foreign policy powers between Congress and the president, Congress has largely surrendered its foreign policy role to the president.
- Recently gridlock and partisan wrangling have led to the charge that Congress is 'the broken branch'.

The presidency

The key issues addressed in this section are:
- constitutional powers
- the growth of presidential power
- relationship with Congress
- relationship with the federal bureaucracy
- the 'two presidencies'
- the office of vice-president

Constitutional powers

The history of English executive despotism, which had led to the revolution and the War of Independence, meant that there were considerable reservations among the framers of the US Constitution over the empowerment of an executive leader. This was to some extent offset, however, by the recognition of the need for an effective executive branch which could turn the 13 constituent states into one functioning entity, after the disorder which had characterised the period of the Articles of Confederation. The compromise was the creation of a single executive, but not one which was intended to exercise popular-based political leadership or to have a popular mandate; to this end, the president was not to be directly elected by the people but only indirectly via the Electoral College. The constitution clearly envisages the president to be subordinate to Congress, which has the role of the principal initiator of legislation, and Article 2, section 3 refers to the president suggesting legislation only 'from time to time'.

The president's powers are nearly all set out in Article 2, and in keeping with the principle of checks and balances, the more significant ones are all checkable by Congress. In section 2 of Article 2, the powers are:
- commander-in-chief of the armed forces — Congress has the check of the sole power to declare war
- to make treaties — Congress has the check of ratification with a two-thirds majority
- to appoint senior government officials, ambassadors, Supreme Court justices and justices of the lower federal courts — Congress has the check of confirmation

The only powers in section 2 without a congressional check are:
- to require in writing the opinion of the principal officer of each of the executive departments
- to grant pardons

In section 3 the president's powers are:
- to make the State of the Union speech and recommend legislation 'from time to time' — Congress has the check of rejecting such legislation
- to take care that the laws 'be faithfully executed' — Congress has the check of the total control of revenue and expenditure

Examiner tip

Any question about the president will need a detailed knowledge of the powers allocated to the office in the constitution, so make sure you are clear what they are.

The only powers in section 3 without a congressional check are:

- to convene extraordinary sessions of Congress
- to receive ambassadors

The president's only significant power not in Article 2 is detailed in Article 1, section 7, namely the power to approve or veto legislation (although the term 'veto' is not itself used); if the president wishes to veto a bill, he or she has to send the legislation back to Congress with a letter explaining why; Congress has the check of an override, albeit requiring a two-thirds majority in both houses.

The growth of presidential power

Reasons

Two key events, the Great Depression and the Cold War, led to the status and power of the modern presidency.

Congressional government

In accordance with the intent of the constitution, the eighteenth and nineteenth centuries were largely periods of congressional government, and the president was for most of the time dependent on the use of the veto to exercise influence.

However, as the economy industrialised and society become more complex and interdependent, the need for national leadership and policy-making became apparent. The institutional structure of Congress meant it was too divided to provide consistent and coordinated leadership, and the president was the only nationally elected office able to meet this need.

The start of the activist presidency

The concept of the activist presidency began with Teddy Roosevelt and Woodrow Wilson at the beginning of the twentieth century; both presidents operated on the basis that the president could do everything that was not specifically prohibited him and that he was not confined by the powers specifically allocated in the constitution.

Knowledge check 27

Who served longer as president, Teddy Roosevelt or Woodrow Wilson?

The passage by Congress in 1921 of the Budget and Accounting Act created the Bureau of the Budget as part of the executive branch, and gave it the responsibility for compiling a single federal budget proposal. This was a recognition, first, that federal spending was now at a level which needed effective central coordination, and, second, of the overall presidential control of domestic policy.

The Great Depression

However, it was the Great Depression in the 1930s which saw the balance of legislative power shift decisively and irrevocably to the president. The dire nature of the situation created the need for the federal government to have a much more active and interventionist role than it had played hitherto. The formulation of broad and coherent policy programmes, and the rescue of a complex industrial economy, were beyond the disparate and parochial operation of Congress. The programme of policies known as the New Deal, which President Roosevelt initiated, extended the reach of the president and the executive branch into the management of the economy, and substantially increased the size of the federal bureaucracy through the creation of bodies such as the Securities and Exchange Commission and the National Labour Board.

The Cold War

Just as the Great Depression expanded the president's powers domestically, so the emergence of the USA after the Second World War as one of two global superpowers had the same effect in foreign policy. For a period before the war Congress had played a significant role in shaping foreign policy — for example, through the passage of the Neutrality Acts — but it was now the president, as head of one of two global superpowers and the 'leader of the free world', who assumed unambiguous control of foreign policy.

President Truman set the precedent of the president taking significant military action through his power as commander-in-chief with only informal consultation with Congress when he ordered military forces to Korea in 1950, in response to the invasion of the South by the Soviet-backed forces of the North. The postwar period also saw the creation of what has become known as the 'national security state'; the 1947 National Security Act created the National Security Council (NSC) and the Central Intelligence Agency (CIA), and reorganised the military into the Department of Defense, with its headquarters in the Pentagon in Virginia. After Korea, the armed forces were no longer mobilised and then demobilised to meet a specific threat, but were expanded and became permanent to counter Soviet aggression, reporting to the president as commander-in-chief. As significantly, the president assumed responsibility for the deployment of the nuclear deterrent, which rapidly became a vital factor in the Cold War.

Methods

Constitutional

The constitutional basis for the expansion of the president's role was partly his explicit power as commander-in-chief and partly the powers implied through the two key clauses in Article Two: 'executive power shall be vested in the president' and '... shall take care that the laws be faithfully executed'. These clauses in the constitution have proved to be sufficiently vague to act as the basis for presidential expansionism and, once the popular vote was established as the means of election, enabled the president to claim a national mandate as the only nationally elected politician.

Institutional support

The Executive Office of the President was created in 1939 after the report of the Brownlow Committee and has grown rapidly since.

Media

Television and film have given rise to a cult of the presidency. Both fictional and actual presidents have been portrayed as ever-present, all-powerful figures; the weekly radio address, began by President Roosevelt, established a direct link between the president and the public; and the constant images of presidential power, such as the White House, the Oval Office, Air Force One and Marine Helicopter, all create a glamorous aura around the office.

Knowledge check 28

What were the Neutrality Acts?

Head of state and party leader

The combination of the roles of head of government, head of state and party leader is an asset for the president. His role as head of state means that Americans have a respect for the office of president which exceeds that given, for example, to a UK prime minister. Americans want their president to be a success, almost irrespective of partisan loyalty, and a presidential appeal to the public and even opposition politicians will — traditionally at any rate — be listened to with respect. As party leader, he has the support of his party during elections and then, to some extent, from his party's representatives and senators in Congress.

The 'imperial presidency'

The power of the presidency grew to such an extent in the postwar period that in the early 1970s, Arthur Schlesinger coined the term 'the imperial presidency', suggesting that the president had cast aside the checks and balances of the system, and was now governing like an emperor. The record of the Nixon presidency, which abroad had conducted a secret war in Cambodia, and at home had refused to spend money mandated by Congress, seemed to provide plenty of support for his thesis. However, Nixon's record provoked a fairly swift congressional reaction in the War Powers Act and the Budget and Impoundment Control Act, intended to rein in what were seen as his abuses of the system. Then, only a year after the publication of Schlesinger's book, Nixon resigned in disgrace. The reassertion of Congress was such that Gerald Ford was referring only a few years later to the 'imperilled presidency', and during the 1980s and 1990s Congress carried out its role of presidential checking with sufficient vigour for the debate over any imperial aspirations of the president to largely die away.

Knowledge check 29

What was the Budget and Impoundment Control Act?

The debate revived to some extent during the presidency of George W. Bush:

- The vice-president Dick Cheney who, as President Ford's chief of staff, had had an insider's view of the 'imperilled presidency', came into office with the explicit intention of strengthening the executive branch. He was quoted in the press as claiming that the period after the Watergate scandal and the Vietnam War was 'the nadir of the modern presidency in terms of authority and legitimacy' and had 'harmed the chief executive's ability to lead in a complicated, dangerous era.'
- The terrorist attacks of September 2001 led the president to take a series of measures, including the detention of US citizens indefinitely as enemy combatants and a National Security Agency (NSA) surveillance programme of US citizens, which critics claimed operated outside congressional checks and oversight, and even the rule of law.

However, as serious as the concerns over these programmes were, the bigger picture is that they were confined to a narrow range of national security issues, and that President Bush's last 2 years in office were conducted as a lame duck with a Democratic Congress. Even on national security, the administration was checked by a succession of Supreme Court cases, such as *Hamdan* v *Rumsfeld*, which held that the military commissions it had created to try Guantanamo Bay detainees were unlawful. In any event, whatever the imperial elements of the Bush presidency, the debate has again subsided since the inauguration of President Obama in 2009.

Knowledge check 30

Why has the debate over the imperial presidency largely subsided since the inauguration of President Obama?

Relationship with Congress

The most crucial relationship for the president is with Congress. From the early twentieth century onwards, the president has set the political agenda and the rest of the system is left to respond to it. However, the nature of a fragmented system with shared powers means that the president cannot act alone, and is dependent on other parts of the system to achieve his goals. The relationship with Congress is particularly important, as constitutionally the president requires the assent of Congress for all legislation, money, appointments and treaties — pretty much everything, in fact.

A significant factor in this relationship is the traditional lack of party discipline in Congress. The separation of powers means that congressmen and -women stand on their own record for re-election, and their willingness to support the president will depend on how far that support will aid their own re-election prospects. This means that the discipline which characterises the UK House of Commons is absent from both the House and the Senate, and the president cannot automatically count on the support of even members of his own party. The healthcare legislation passed in 2010 showed that even the president's 'own' members of Congress will resist him, if a vote against his proposals will play better with the voters at home. Consequently, the president cannot order anything to happen, and the successful pursuit of his goals will require bargaining, compromising, and the creation of coalitions to bring it about: hence the famous summary of presidential power, 'the power to persuade.'

Knowledge check 31

What is 'pork'? What and where is the 'Bridge to Nowhere'?

Factors which can affect the president's relationship with Congress

Popularity

High approval poll ratings give the president increased authority, and may create a political cost for members of Congress opposing a popular president. Conversely, poor ratings, certainly below 40%, will weaken the president's authority and impose limited costs at worst on congressional opposition. President Bush was at below 40% for much of his second term, and poor ratings blighted the prospects of his second-term agenda. Even a special election defeat for the president's party, such as that suffered by the Democrats in Ted Kennedy's Massachusetts Senate seat in January 2010, may reduce the president's leverage.

Knowledge check 32

What were the circumstances of the Massachusetts special election in 2010?

In connection with the Bush presidency, however, it is worth pointing out that even with the president's approval ratings in the low 30s, the principal cause of which was Iraq, Congress was unable to effect any significant change in Iraq policy; the 'surge' was announced in January 2007 after the election of a Democratic Congress pledged to reduce troop numbers, and the only bill passed by both houses to change policy was vetoed by the president.

Partisanship

There is no doubt that the president is in a much stronger position with his own party controlling both houses of Congress than not, and the larger the majority the better. However, although party control may be significant, it is certainly not sufficient to guarantee trouble-free passage for the president's legislation. Recent history suggests that Republican Congresses are generally more supportive of a Republican president than a Democratic Congress of a Democratic president. President Clinton from 1993 until 1995, and President Obama from 2009 until 2011, both found difficulties passing key legislation through chambers controlled by their own party.

As a generally more partisan chamber, the House will usually be more supportive of its own president than the Senate, though even there not always consistently. For example, although President Bush was able to rely on a solid House majority on economic issues such as tax cuts, it proved less solid on social issues such as medicare and the No Child Left Behind legislation, and he was forced in both cases to rely on Democratic support.

The experience of the Clinton presidency from 1995 to 2001 with a Republican Congress also suggests divided government is by no means a complete disadvantage. It is inevitable that a president arriving in office with his 'own' Congress suffers from unrealistic expectations as to what is achievable in the 2 years of its life. For all that President Obama did secure Congress's approval for in the period 2009–11, a number of constituencies — perhaps principal among them the Latino community — were unhappy that their demands were not translated into legislation. With a Congress controlled by the opposition, the president benefits from reduced expectations and from no longer having to disappoint one or more elements of his coalition.

First-/second-term president

There is a marked contrast between the dynamic of the president's first and second terms. In the first term, members of Congress of the president's party are aware that, in all probability, the president will be the party's nominee in the next election, and, to some extent at least, public perception of his performance, and the existence or otherwise of presidential 'coat-tails', will have an impact on their own re-election prospects. They therefore have some incentive to make that perception positive.

This incentive largely disappears in the second term and the likelihood of their support diminishes. The presidential 'lame-duck' period is officially the president's period in office after the election of a new president in November until his inauguration on 20 January. However, it can start at any point in the second term, particularly after the midterms, which is the last election the president is able to influence significantly.

Importance of events

Unforeseen events can have an influential effect. The Oklahoma City bombings in 1995 occurred at a time when President Clinton was on the defensive against a Republican congressional leadership which was acting like a parliamentary majority, in the House at least. The bombing had the effect of putting the president centre stage and enabled him to regain the initiative.

Means available to the president

The State of the Union speech

In this speech at the beginning of each year, the president has a national audience to whom he can set out his priorities and legislative agenda for the next 12 months.

Knowledge check 33
Why would Republican Congresses be generally more supportive of a Republican president than a Democratic Congress of a Democratic president?

Knowledge check 34
What were the government shutdowns of the 1990s?

Knowledge check 35
What were the disappointments of the Latino community with the Obama first term?

Knowledge check 36
What are presidential 'coat-tails'?

Patronage

Although, unlike a UK prime minister, the president cannot offer jobs in the executive in return for the support of members of Congress, he does have a variety of other inducements.

A presidential visit to help with fundraising is of significant value to a member of Congress. Senators and representatives are as much in thrall to the trappings of presidential power as anyone else, and an invitation to the White House to watch a football game in the film theatre, or a flight on Air Force One, are attractive propositions. The press reported that in March 2010 the president invited representatives Dennis Kucinich and Marcia Fudge onto Air Force One for a flight to Ohio to press the case for health reform.

Personnel

The White House staff, members of the cabinet and the vice-president all become involved in pushing the president's legislative agenda through Congress. In the negotiations to secure the renewal of the Bush-era tax cuts in December 2010, the vice-president was both shoring up the support of congressional Democrats and negotiating directly with Republican leaders, while White House staff with a stake in the proposals, such as economic adviser Gene Sperling, the Office of Management and Budget (OMB) director Jack Lew, and Treasury Secretary Timothy Geithner, all lobbied. Even Bill Clinton was brought into the White House briefing room to praise the president's proposals to the assembled ranks of the press.

Personal skills

The president will seek to use his personal powers of charm and persuasion on individual members of Congress. In the 2010 tax renewal negotiations, the president called or met with reportedly dozens of Senate and House Democrats. Former senators, who are at home in the culture of Washington, have usually proved more adept at this than ex-governors; President Johnson carried over much of his operational manner as Senate majority leader into the White House, to which President Carter never adapted.

The 'bully pulpit'

The term 'bully pulpit' was first coined by Teddy Roosevelt and is a recognition of the president's ability to use the status and power of his office to frame the debate and pressure members of Congress via their constituents. The president can exploit the fact that whatever he does is newsworthy and will generate media coverage. The bully pulpit can be used in a number of ways: for example, a straightforward televised national address, or the president can take his message 'on the road' through a series of highly publicised local town hall meetings.

Power of veto

The use of the veto has changed in recent years. In the earlier part of the twentieth century, the veto was used extensively — President Roosevelt famously vetoed 635 bills in total — and it was a principal means of asserting executive power when the executive was relatively weak. It is now used more sparingly, and tends to be seen as a sign of weakness. Its use suggests that the president has lost control of the agenda, if Congress is willing to pass legislation in defiance of his stated preferences, especially if Congress is controlled by the president's party. However, in the later stages of a presidency, or when faced by a Congress controlled by the opposition party, the veto may be the only way a president has of exerting influence.

That said, a lack of presidential vetoes may not necessarily be a sign of strength either. The first 5½ years of the Bush presidency saw no vetoes at all until the veto of the Stem Cell Research Enhancement Act in July 2006, an unprecedentedly long period. This was seen by sympathisers as the product of the president's domination. However, critics saw it either as the product of indifference, when the president should have been keeping the budget under control, or as the president misguidedly wanting to project an image of strength and seeing the veto as inconsistent with the image of a powerful, agenda-setting leadership.

Ways around Congress

The president has a variety of means he can adopt to work round any obstruction he encounters in Congress.

Recess appointments

The president can avoid the need for the Senate's confirmation of appointments by making a recess appointment. They are by no means a complete solution, since they only last for the life of the Congress, i.e. a maximum of 2 years and probably less, but the president can make a recess appointment in the hope that the next elections will result in a Congress more favourably disposed to his nominee. President Bush appointed John Bolton to UN ambassador in 2005 during a congressional recess after his nomination was filibustered twice in the Senate.

Knowledge check 39

What ultimately happened to John Bolton's nomination as UN ambassador?

White House appointments

Appointments to the White House staff do not require Senate confirmation and some so-called 'czars' exercise more influence than their equivalent in the cabinet.

Knowledge check 40

What are 'czars'?

Executive orders

Executive orders are directives aimed at the federal bureaucracy, and give guidance on the implementation of laws passed by Congress. They are not explicitly defined in the constitution and the legitimate extent of their use is unclear; critics complain that they often amount to the creation of new policy. More usually, they concern routine matters, but they can be in controversial or significant areas of policy. President Clinton, for example, lifted the ban on gay people in the military through executive order, and President Bush imposed restrictions on stem cell research, which lasted until President Obama lifted them through the same means.

Executive orders are a potent instrument. Unlike legislative proposals, if the president acts unilaterally, in the absence of a congressional or judicial response, the order assumes the status of law. Both responses do occur, but congressional legislation is difficult to pass and the judiciary typically defers to the president. However, if an

Content guidance

order requires appropriations, Congress can introduce amendments and restrictions and, ultimately though rarely, executive orders can be successfully challenged in the courts, as happened to President Truman's order nationalising the steel mills in *Youngstown* v *Sawyer*.

Executive agreements

Executive agreements with other countries can be used instead of treaties. The cumbersome and demanding requirements for treaty ratification mean that agreements are used far more extensively than treaties, especially after the Second World War when America's influence spread round the globe. More than 2,800 executive agreements were made in the Reagan administration alone. Attempts to rein in the use of executive agreements have been largely unsuccessful; two Supreme Court cases, *United States* v *Belmont* (1937) and *United States* v *Pink* (1942) upheld the right of the president to make executive agreements and, although the Case-Zablocki Act 1972 required the Secretary of State to report to Congress any international agreement made other than by treaty within 60 days, virtually every subsequent presidency has circumvented its requirements. However, executive agreements are not binding on succeeding administrations, so significant change with long-term consequences still requires a full treaty.

Signing statements

Signing statements are official documents in which the president gives his legal interpretation of a bill for the federal bureaucracy to follow when implementing the new law. They became a particular source of controversy during the presidency of George W. Bush. The president repeatedly asserted his right to ignore those sections of bills which, in his view, unconstitutionally infringed his authority as president. In his statement on the amendment initiated by Senator John McCain banning the torture of suspected terrorists, the president undertook to implement it '...in a manner consistent with the constitutional authority of the president', which was widely taken to mean that it would not be implemented at all.

Relationship with the federal bureaucracy

The second crucial relationship for the president is with the federal bureaucracy. The federal bureaucracy is the term used to refer to what would be regarded in the UK as the American civil service. It has the functions of a traditional civil service, namely to implement the legislation passed by Congress and the instructions of the president, and to advise on the formulation of new policy. It also has the traditional power of a civil service, magnified by the size of the American economy, and the federal budget for 2010 was in the region of $3.5 trillion. The reach of the federal government expanded throughout the twentieth century, accelerated sharply by the New Deal and Great Society, and federal programmes and regulation now impact on almost every aspect of American life.

The significance of the federal bureaucracy for the president is that it is the bureaucracy which is responsible for converting his policies into action, the success of which will directly reflect on him.

Knowledge check 41

Why did President Truman want to nationalise the steel mills?

Problems of control

There are a number of issues which inhibit effective presidential control of the bureaucracy. First, there are issues which are common to the relationship between all elected politicians and their bureaucracies:

- The bureaucracy has experience and expertise in its area of operation which is unlikely to be matched by any elected politician or their personal advisers; it has access to and control of information; and it is made up for the most part of permanent career civil servants who can stall policy change while waiting for a change of administration.
- A bureaucracy has its own interests which do not coincide with its political masters; it will promote policies which are best able to further its own goals of survival and expansion; and it has limited interest in the overall national interest, or in pursuing policies which threaten the status quo.
- It is aided in the pursuit of these goals by the nature of legislation which in places will be vague or ambiguous, and the implementation of which requires interpretation by the bureaucracy. Even if it is not always implemented in the narrow interests of the bureaucracy, it may well cause difficulties or embarrassment for the president.

Second, there are more specific issues:

- **Divided loyalties:** The bureaucracy is part of the executive branch and its function is to serve the president, but it is dependent on Congress for its continued existence and funding. Congress has the power of oversight of its activities, and to establish, merge or abolish federal departments. In addition, the power of incumbency means members of Congress are likely to be around much longer than the president, so bureaucrats have a strong incentive to pay as much or more attention to the wishes of Congress as to those of the president. Notoriously, the bureaucracy can form alliances with congressional committees and pressure groups to form 'iron triangles' — these work against the public interest in maintaining programmes of benefit to all three points of the triangle but hardly anyone else. However, not even the most lucrative triangle can resist presidential pressure for ever, and one such came to an end with the cancellation of the F22 fighter programme by the Obama administration.
- **Lack of coordination:** Multiple agencies, for example, have a stake in foreign policy: the State Department, the Defense Department, the NSC and the CIA, to name just some of the most prominent. All have different priorities and sometimes pull in different directions. In particular, there is a long history of tension between State and Defense Departments, which was highly visible, for example, during the first term of the Bush presidency in the rivalry between secretaries Powell and Rumsfeld.

Presidential resources

The president has a number of resources at his disposal to control the bureaucracy.

Cabinet

The cabinet consists of all the heads of executive departments, plus an assortment of others, including the vice-president and the White House chief of staff. The heads of the executive departments are all presidential appointees and, although they need Senate confirmation, they are rarely rejected; no nomination has been rejected since John Tower's nomination for Defense Secretary in 1989, although a number since

> **Knowledge check 42**
>
> What is an 'iron triangle'?

Knowledge check 43

Why was John Tower's nomination for Defense Secretary rejected?

Examiner tip

Questions will often ask candidates to contrast the roles and effectiveness of the cabinet and EOP, so be clear about the differences between them.

have dropped out in the preliminary stages of the confirmation process, such as Tom Daschle, who was President Obama's initial choice for health secretary.

As a tool of governing, the cabinet has limitations. There is no tradition of collective decision making, and to an even greater extent than in the UK, cabinet secretaries are representatives of their departments, with probably little to contribute to other areas of policy making. The president will have had to consider a number of factors in choosing his cabinet, of which knowledge and competence will be only two. The cabinet has a symbolic function as much as any other, and a key consideration in its selection will be the need to make it representative, both of different wings of the president's party, and of America itself, in gender, race and region.

Executive Office of the President (EOP)

The EOP was set up in 1939 as a result of the Brownlow Committee recommendations, which recognised that the president was in need of more support; prior to the Second World War, the president had authority to hire only four staff aides above clerical rank.

Originally, the EOP comprised just the White House Office and the Bureau of the Budget, and other units such as the Council of Economic Advisers (1946) and the National Security Council (1947) were added subsequently. It now has around 2,000 employees and a budget of several hundred million dollars. It provides support for the president in policy development and presentation, and has a less symbolic and more overtly political role than the cabinet, although only very few EOP staff, for example the director of the Office of Management and Budget, need Senate confirmation.

Within the EOP, the White House staff form the president's key advisers, instantly recognisable to followers of *The West Wing*. The organisation and responsibilities of these staff vary considerably from president to president. The chief of staff, as the highest-ranking member of the EOP, is responsible for ensuring that it meets the president's needs; with a 'hands-off' president, this person may become a quasi-prime minister, as was the case with James Baker and Donald Regan during the Reagan presidency. Since the Nixon/Kissinger era, the national security adviser (NSA) has been increasingly influential in foreign policy relative to the State Department, but foreign policy in George W. Bush's first term was dominated by the Cheney–Rumsfeld partnership and Condoleezza Rice as NSA was relatively subordinate.

Appointment

Unlike in the UK, where the prime minister inherits a permanent civil service and can appoint only a small number of personal advisers, the president has power over several thousand appointments and can ensure political sympathisers are in key posts. However, this is to some extent outweighed by the need to balance political loyalty and competence, and the president may find it difficult to find suitably experienced appointees from the campaign supporters who expect to be rewarded.

Reorganisation

Presidential reorganisation of the bureaucracy depends on the approval of Congress, which will have its own priorities, very often not coinciding with the president's own. The most recent major reorganisation centred on the creation of the Department of Homeland Security in 2002, and is illustrative of the problems the president may face. Initially, President Bush favoured an office within the EOP headed by a Homeland Security Adviser, and resisted public and congressional pressure for a government department. When he finally relented, there followed a prolonged battle between the president and congressional Democrats, in particular over the employment terms of employees of the new department. This was finally resolved, largely in the president's favour, only after the president had campaigned on the issue in the 2002 midterms.

The 'two presidencies'

The term 'two presidencies' was coined in the 1960s by Aaron Wildavsky as a pithy summary of the thesis that there exists a marked difference in scale between the constraints operating on the president in domestic and in foreign policy. As already outlined, the constraints on the president domestically are considerable, whereas, in some respects at least, he can operate as much more of a free agent abroad. The 'invitation to struggle' between the president and Congress for control of foreign policy has been won by the president who, since the Second World War especially, has assumed control for the overall direction of foreign policy. Congress will usually defer to the president, particularly during periods of perceived threat to the USA. There may be attempts at congressional assertion at other times but, especially in the use of the forces, the president's position as commander-in-chief gives him the upper hand. If the president initiates military action, Congress will rarely have the inclination or the ability to offer an effective or even coherent challenge.

Department of Homeland Security
The creation of the Department of Homeland Security was the most far-reaching of the Bush administration's domestic responses to the attacks of September 2001. It brought together a wide variety of federal agencies previously dispersed in other departments, in an attempt to better coordinate anti-terrorist activities, and is now the third largest federal department.

Congress and Libya

The congressional response to the president's deployment of American forces in the action against Libya in the summer of 2011 was characteristic. The president did not seek congressional approval at the beginning of the operation, and then claimed that, since there were no ground troops involved, and American forces were largely involved in a supportive role, the action did not constitute 'hostilities' as the term is used in the War Powers Act. Consequently, the requirement of the Act to seek congressional approval for military action within 60 days did not apply.

In the face of this brush-off, Congress floundered; the Senate became so divided over the issue that, after an initial vote in March calling for the possible establishment of a no-fly zone over Libya, it then proved impossible even to formulate a resolution to vote on. Several members of the House were vociferous in their condemnation of the president, and Denis Kucinich at one point called for his impeachment. Nevertheless, in a series of votes, the House failed to make any meaningful impact on policy, voting on the same day both against authorising the use of American forces and refusing to limit funding for the mission. It was reminiscent of the House votes on the action in Kosovo in 1999, when the House was famously described by a White House spokesman as voting '...no on going forward, no on going back, and they tied on standing still'.

Notwithstanding congressional impotence, even in military deployments the president is by no means a completely free agent:

- Since the Vietnam War, presidents have been very aware of public opinion and the electoral consequences of adverse reaction to casualties. These apply particularly in a president's first term, but even towards the end of his presidency, President Clinton was cautious about the deployment of ground troops in Kosovo. President Obama set a time limit on the 'surge' in Afghanistan in 2010 to reassure the public that he was not making an open-ended commitment, which, in the view of many commentators, significantly undercut its purpose.
- As a civilian, the president is partly dependent on the advice on strategy of his top military commanders; this relationship may become strained, as it was for much of the Clinton presidency, which began with a more or less open revolt among the joint chiefs of staff over the proposed relaxation of the ban on homosexuals serving in the military.
- The Supreme Court will usually defer to the commander-in-chief, and rarely even agrees to hear cases with a foreign policy basis. However, George W. Bush suffered several setbacks at the hands of the court and, for example, the military tribunals set up to try Guantanamo suspects were declared unlawful in *Hamdan* v *Rumsfeld* in 2006.

The existence of meaningful constraints is even more apparent in areas of foreign policy outside military action, and foreign governments and their offshoots in particular will attempt to exert pressure on the direction of foreign policy. The power of the Israel lobby has been well chronicled, and in recent years especially, any attempt by the president to cajole Israel into policies it sees as antipathetic to its interests will be met with a coordinated response in Congress. President Obama's call in 2011 for a two-state solution that restored Israel's borders to their pre-1967 positions was not favourably received by Israel or its allies in America; it was followed in very short order by an invited speech by the Israeli Prime Minister Netanyahu before Congress, which was interrupted by bipartisan standing ovations 29 times. In the face of this level of opposition, the administration's ambitions for the two-state solution have limited prospects of success.

Knowledge check 44

What is the Israel lobby?

Vice-president

Status

Despite the alleged rigidity of the constitution, the office of vice-president, much like almost every aspect of the US system of government, has been in a state of almost constant evolution for the last 200 years. Although the powers accorded the office in the constitution are modest, its recent history has been one of steadily increasing influence, markedly so in the second half of the twentieth century. The reasons for this include the following:

- The vast expansion in the reach of the federal government has made it almost essential for the president to be able to delegate some responsibility to the vice-president. The vice-president has become central to the administration, and he now is a member of the cabinet and has an office in the West Wing. Under President Clinton, for example, Al Gore was involved in promoting environmental initiatives and the greater use of new technology, and was responsible for the National Partnership for Reinventing Government, a flagship project to increase government efficiency.

- The rise of partisan government in Congress has made it vital for the president to maintain or create party majorities in one or preferably both houses. Vice-presidents have frequently had more congressional experience than the president, and this has given them a key role, both in maintaining party loyalty in the existing Congress, and in fundraising and campaigning to increase party representation in the next.
- Since the ratification of the 22nd Amendment in 1951, formally limiting the president to two terms, the vice-president has almost always been seen as the 'president in waiting'. No vice-president since then has lost a primary election to become their party's nominee, and four have gone on to be president, although only George H. W. Bush in 1988 actually won the presidential election immediately following his term as vice-president.

22nd Amendment This amendment incorporated into the constitution the convention that presidents should serve no more than two terms. The catalyst for its adoption was the breach of this convention by President Roosevelt's election for four consecutive terms, starting in 1932.

Formal powers

The formal powers allocated to the vice-president by the constitution and its amendments are relatively few:

- to be the presiding officer of the Senate, although by convention the vice-president rarely attends
- to break a tied vote in the Senate, a power which has been used on some crucial votes in the recent past, such as Al Gore's vote in 1993 to pass the president's budget
- to count and then announce the votes of the Electoral College; famously, Al Gore was required to announce his own defeat
- to assume the office of president should the president die, resign or be otherwise removed
- to act as president should the president make a written declaration to Congress that he is temporarily unable to carry out his duties

The two most recent vice-presidents, Dick Cheney (2001–09) and Joe Biden (2009–), have both made a distinctive contribution to the evolution of the office.

Dick Cheney

The scope of the influence of Dick Cheney on the Bush administration has been well chronicled, and the label of the 'most powerful vice-president in history' is now accepted as the unchallenged orthodoxy. A number of factors contributed to this influence:

- **The closeness of his relationship with the president:** The vice-president had known the Bush family over decades, and was not, unlike Sarah Palin for example, a tactical addition to the ticket of someone who the presidential nominee had barely heard of.
- **His experience in Washington:** Cheney had been part of the Nixon administration, President Ford's chief of staff, a House representative for Wyoming for 10 years, and Defense Secretary under the first President Bush, and this range of experience, especially when contrasted with the new president's almost complete inexperience, made him indispensable.

- **His extensive contacts throughout the bureaucracy and the EOP:** The vice-president was part of a network of like-minded conservatives, including, at the top of the administration, Donald Rumsfeld as Defense Secretary and Paul Wolfowitz as his deputy.
- **His lack of ambition:** The vice-president's lack of presidential ambition meant that at no stage did he have to consider how either his decisions or the president's would play in a future election.

Whereas previous recent vice-presidents had tended to concentrate on a few specific areas of policy, Cheney ranged across the entire administration:

- He had been concerned about the erosion of presidential power after Watergate, and vigorously promoted its expansion, particularly after the attacks of September 2001.
- He personally promoted the use of unauthorised surveillance, robust interrogation techniques and the creation of military commissions to try prisoners.
- He was closely involved in administration plans to invade Iraq.
- He oversaw lists of potential Supreme Court nominees.
- He shaped and pushed through the Bush tax cuts, overcoming the resistance of both Alan Greenspan (who was worried, probably correctly, about the effects of tax cuts on the deficit) and the president himself to a policy of tax breaks for the wealthy.
- He constantly sought to relax or simply ignore environmental regulations to favour business, either through direct intervention or by the placing of sympathisers in key positions.

For all Cheney's utility and ubiquity, there is little doubt that his influence diminished in the Bush second term. His ability to attract unfavourable media coverage, epitomised by the hunting accident of 2006, earned him the sobriquet of the 'Velcro Veep'. His claim, reported in 2007, that he was not required to lodge documents with the National Archive office because he was not part of the executive branch was seen by many commentators as bizarre, and reinforced an image of obsessive secrecy and unaccountability.

Knowledge check 45

What was the significance of the sobriquet of the 'Velcro Veep'?

As an architect of the invasion of Iraq, Cheney's stock declined as the situation there failed to show significant improvement, and he suffered from the loss of allies such as Rumsfeld and Wolfowitz, and the rise of the influence of the State Department under Condoleezza Rice. The vice-president was sidelined in negotiations with North Korea over its nuclear weapons programme in 2007, which produced an agreement disapproved of by many conservatives (and, it was speculated, by Cheney as well) as rewarding North Korea. By his own account, he failed to persuade the president to launch a bombing mission on a suspected Syrian nuclear reactor in 2007.

Joe Biden

With his 30+ years of experience in the Senate, Joe Biden was as much a Washington insider as Dick Cheney, but in personality and image he presented very differently. Biden came across as far more affable and willing to please. As a sitting senator, he was a more conventional choice for the presidential ticket than Cheney had been and, as an Eastern senator and chairman of the Senate Foreign Relations Committee, he was a complement to Barack Obama.

Knowledge check 46

Why was Joe Biden a complement to Barack Obama?

Biden could not hope to (and probably did not want to) maintain the level of influence exerted by Cheney in President Bush's first term, and he had to some extent to redefine the role. Initially, the vice-president's tendency to garrulousness and fondness for straight-talking (on one trip he called a Wisconsin custard shop manager a 'smartass') made him seem something of a liability to the administration, and he remained the constant butt of the late-night comedians. Nevertheless, he proved his usefulness in a variety of ways:

- His candour made him seem more of a man of the people, and gave him a wider appeal than the sometimes rather cerebral and detached persona of the president.
- Especially after the departure of Rahm Emanuel, he had an unmatched range of contacts and understanding of Congress. He proved an invaluable negotiator on a series of vital administration measures, including the extension of the Bush tax cuts, the START treaty and the raising of the debt ceiling.
- On foreign policy in particular, he contributed vigorously to policy debate, and played an important role in discussion on the surge in Afghanistan as the principal sceptic of the policy of escalation favoured by the military.
- He also fulfilled the traditional functions of the vice-president. He has been the champion of specific policy areas, such as high-speed rail, for which, as a long-time commuter, he has a special affinity, and an active fundraiser for Democratic candidates. *Politico* wrote in June 2011 that 'Fundraising has replaced funerals as the leading vice-presidential pursuit' — and the vice-president had by then already attended over 150 events.

Summary

- The constitutional powers of the president are extensive, but are nearly all checkable by Congress.
- Throughout the twentieth century, the power of the president has grown in response to the need for coordinated leadership both at home and abroad.
- The constitutional system of checks means that successful management of the president's relationship with Congress is crucial, although there are a variety of means the president can use to avoid congressional restraints.
- The federal bureaucracy is responsible for implementing policy, and the president needs to ensure it is following his agenda rather than its own.
- The term 'the two presidencies' is used to reflect the different levels of restraint the president experiences at home and in foreign policy.

The Supreme Court

The key issues addressed in this section are:
- the role of the court
- the appointment process
- judicial interpretation
- the power of the court
- a political or judicial body?
- the Roberts Court

The role of the court

Article 3 of the United States Constitution vests 'the judicial Power...in one supreme Court...'. Despite Hamilton's description of the court as 'the least dangerous branch', throughout its history it has made controversial decisions which have shaped American society. It was a Supreme Court decision, *Dred Scott*, which led to the Civil War, and in the twentieth century the decisions in *Brown* and *Roe* have set the political agenda until the present day. However, arguments persist over the legitimacy of the role of the Supreme Court in the political system and, perhaps in consequence, the court has a profile and even glamour which stands in contrast to the sober anonymity of the UK judiciary. The justices are well-known personalities who regularly attract comment and controversy in the press, and the confirmation process has come to justify the term 'media circus'.

Procedure

The Supreme Court is primarily an *appellate* court, meaning nearly all the cases it hears are appeals from lower courts.

It receives several thousand requests for hearings every year, but in recent years a writ of *certiorari* (meaning the court agrees to hear the case) has been granted to fewer than 100 annually.

Reasons for the court agreeing to hear a case include the following:
- The case is considered to have significant implications for the constitution or society as a whole.
- There have been conflicting lower court opinions.
- There has been a request from the federal government.

Verdicts are reached by majority decision, and only a bare majority is required, i.e. 5–4 is sufficient on the current composition of nine. However, given that a divided court implies uncertainty and suggests the possibility of future reversals, justices will always seek unanimity.

Judicial review

The status and influence of the court derives from the power it has over the constitution. This power — known as 'judicial review' — means that the court is able to decide whether congressional and state legislation, and the actions of the executive branch, are in accordance with the constitution; if they are not, the court can 'strike down' anything which it judges to be unconstitutional.

One reason the power of the court is controversial is that judicial review is not explicitly granted in the constitution, but was awarded by the court to itself in a case heard in 1803, *Marbury* v *Madison*. Chief Justice Marshall, who wrote the court's opinion, argued that a power to decide whether the other branches have contravened the constitution must be implicit in the nature of the constitution as higher law; if a law of Congress can contravene the constitution, then the constitution clearly cannot be higher law, and it loses its role as a statement of fundamental principles, and indeed its very purpose. If that point is conceded, then — since the constitution *is* law, and the constitution gives judges the role of interpreting the law — the judgement of whether the constitution has been contravened must belong with the judiciary.

This reasoning has not impressed critics, among them Thomas Jefferson, the third president and the principal author of the Declaration of Independence, who wrote in 1820 that to '...consider the judges as the ultimate arbiters of all constitutional questions is a very dangerous doctrine indeed'. However, given that the constitution does not provide any other procedure for resolving disputes over constitutionality, judicial review has survived.

Knowledge check 47

Why has the Supreme Court such an important role in US politics?

Judicial independence

The independence of the court from the other branches is maintained through:
- the separation of powers — the judicial function is the exclusive power of the judicial branch
- the appointment of justices, not election
- lifetime tenure of justices, who are only removable through impeachment
- the fact that justices' pay cannot be reduced during their period in office

Liberals v Conservatives

The key recent development in the composition of the court has been the emergence of a liberal/conservative divide.

After the Second World War, the court increasingly took on cases concerning civil rights, and cases concerning controversial issues such as abortion and capital punishment. Beginning with *Brown* v *Topeka Board of Education* (1954), which led to the desegregation of schools, the court made a series of decisions, among them:
- *Loving* v *Virginia* (1967), striking down state bans on interracial marriage
- *Swann* v *Charlotte Mecklenburg Board of Education* (1971), sanctioning busing
- *Roe* v *Wade* (1973), creating a constitutional right for a woman to obtain an abortion

These cases had the effect of strengthening the rights of groups such as women and ethnic minorities, who had arguably not been adequately represented by the other branches of government.

Conservatives saw these decisions as the court misreading the constitution to create rights which were never intended by the framers, and to impose its own liberal values on areas which were rightfully the responsibility of the state governments.

Since the 1970s and the decision in *Roe*, which particularly enraged conservatives, it has become a principal goal of the conservative movement to install sympathetic justices on the court to reverse at least some of these decisions, and of liberals to do likewise to defend them.

The appointment process

The number of justices has been fixed at nine since the 1860s. The procedure for their appointment is laid out in Article 2 of the constitution; when a vacancy arises, it is filled by the president 'with the Advice and Consent of the Senate', which in practice means that the president's nomination is required to be confirmed by a Senate majority vote.

The guarantee of lifetime tenure means that the choice of a Supreme Court justice is among the more consequential decisions a president will make, as it offers him the opportunity to influence public policy for years after his own departure.

Factors which influence the president's choice

Judicial philosophy

All nominees come to the nomination process with a conservative or liberal label, acquired through decisions made in lower courts or through their writings. It is accepted as legitimate that a president will seek to nominate a justice with a judicial outlook similar to his own, although of course there is no guarantee that a nominee will conform to their pre-confirmation label once installed on the court. David Souter, nominated by President Bush on the basis that he was a 'home run' for conservatives, became a reliable member of the liberal bloc.

Judicial ability

Although a nominee need never have been a judge, they need to be able to demonstrate that they have a level of judicial credibility. Two recent examples illustrate the point:
- Elena Kagan, who was appointed to the court in 2010, had never served as a judge but had had a distinguished academic legal career, sufficient to have been already nominated (unsuccessfully, as the congressional term expired before she could be confirmed) to the DC circuit appeals court in 1999.
- Harriet Miers, nominated by President Bush in 2005, had also never served as a judge but, in contrast, had no academic record, and did not impress members of the Senate with her grasp of constitutional law. She withdrew from the process amid a flurry of unfavourable coverage.

The composition of the Senate

The president will need to consider the reaction of a Senate controlled by the opposition party. Three nominees have been rejected since the Second World War, and all were Republican nominees rejected by a Democratic-controlled Senate.

Representation of different groups

Here, two considerations will influence the president: first, as an unelected body, the court needs to be seen to be representative of America to maintain its legitimacy and, second, the president may want to send a signal of support to particular groups. Both could be seen at work in President Obama's nomination to the court of Sonia Sotomayor; Latinos had been an important element of his coalition in 2008, and her appointment

Knowledge check 48

Who was the last Supreme Court nominee rejected by the Senate?

also recognised the increasing significance of the Latino population, which had not until then (with the possible exception of Benjamin Cardozo) been represented on the court.

The process

1 The president nominates

When a vacancy arises, through either the death or resignation of one of the nine justices, the first stage of the process lies with the president, who has to choose his nominee. Even when the president has a background in law, as in the case of President Obama, this is likely to involve extensive consultation; according to press reports, Obama called every member of the Senate Judiciary Committee personally when he was deciding whether to nominate Sonia Sotomayor.

2 The Senate considers

The nominee completes an extensive 64-page questionnaire, which is considered by the members of the Senate Judiciary Committee before the formal interviews take place. Although the completion of this questionnaire might be thought to be a formality, Harriet Miers' replies were such that they ultimately led to the withdrawal of her nomination. The Senate Judiciary Committee then conducts an interview of the nominee, and anyone else the committee chooses, extending over several days. The witnesses who are called either to support or to oppose the nomination usually attract little attention; the exception was Anita Hill, whose appearance to oppose Clarence Thomas's nomination in 1991 was the object of intense media interest.

3 The Senate votes

Once the interviews are completed, there are two votes. The first involves just the members of the judiciary committee, and the second the whole Senate. The committee's vote is only recommendatory, but it is a good indicator of the likely outcome in the second vote; Robert Bork's nomination in 1987 was defeated 9–5 in committee, and Clarence Thomas's in 1991 was tied 7–7.

Like all nominations, only a simple majority is required for the confirmation of a justice. It is open to opponents to mount a filibuster, and several circuit Court of Appeals nominations have been blocked in this way in recent years; the nomination of Goodwin Liu to the ninth circuit was filibustered by Republican opponents in May 2011. However, although they have often been threatened, attempted filibusters of Supreme Court nominees are rare (there was an unsuccessful filibuster of Samuel Alito in 2006, which the then Senator Obama supported), and the only successful filibuster defeated the nomination of Abe Fortas, President Johnson's nominee for Chief Justice in 1968.

Problems

The process for the appointment of justices has been increasingly criticised in recent years, on grounds of politicisation and meaninglessness.

Politicisation

As the conservative/liberal divide on the court has deepened, and Congress itself has become more polarised, members of the party opposed to the president will try to

Examiner tip

In a short answer, do not just give a list of points, but indicate which point is most significant overall; in the case of Supreme Court nominees, for example, different presidents may have been influenced by different factors.

Knowledge check 49

Why did Anita Hill's appearance cause such controversy?

bring about the rejection of his nominees, irrespective of their merits. The nomination process has ceased to resemble an objective enquiry; following the confirmation of Elena Kagan, the *Los Angeles Times* wrote that nominees '...are now being treated like contentious pieces of legislation' and quoted a source that 'the era of clearly qualified nominees getting broad bipartisan support in the Senate will officially end with this vote'. Kagan was the third consecutive nominee to receive under 70 votes in support; in contrast, Antonin Scalia was confirmed in 1986 with 98 votes in support and none against, Anthony Kennedy in 1988 with 97 votes for and none against, Ruth Ginsburg in 1993 with 96 votes in support and three against, and Stephen Breyer in 1994 with 87 votes for and nine against.

Accompanying the increased partisanship in the Senate has been an increase in the activities of interest groups. The rejection of the Robert Bork nomination was a success for the liberal groups which campaigned against him (the 'People for the American Way' ad by Gregory Peck can be watched on YouTube). The scale and vigour of the campaign caught conservative groups unawares, but since then both liberal and conservative groups have mounted increasingly expensive campaigns for and against nominees, running TV ads and mobilising supporters to put pressure on their senators. The success of the Bork campaign has not yet been reproduced, however, and even a group as powerful as the NRA, which opposed both the Sotomayor and Kagan nominations, may gain little traction against a well-qualified candidate.

Meaninglessness

The Bork nomination was significant in another way. In his answers to the committee, Bork was, in hindsight, unnecessarily expansive (at least from his own point of view) and told the members, for example, that the decisions in *Roe* v *Wade* 'contain almost no legal reasoning', supplying his opponents with his own ammunition.

Since then, nominees have become much more guarded in their responses, to the extent that, some time before her own nomination, Elena Kagan characterised the proceedings as 'a vapid and hollow charade'. Nominees will frequently decline to answer questions on legal issues, and only advance opinions which are completely uncontroversial, leaving senators and the wider audience with only a hazy sense of how they would perform if confirmed.

Another related issue is justices' almost complete lack of accountability once installed on the court. This has led some senators to discount the little that nominees do say; some of those who heard John Roberts state that it is '...a jolt to the legal system when you overrule a precedent' felt aggrieved when the court he presides over administered just such a jolt in *Citizens United* v *FEC*.

Judicial interpretation

The basis of the division between liberals and conservatives on the court is their different approaches to the interpretation of the constitution. There is no one liberal or one conservative approach to constitutional interpretation, but a number of linked approaches on both sides.

Knowledge check 50

Why do interest groups run ads for and against Supreme Court candidates?

Knowledge check 51

Why are justices unaccountable?

Conservative approaches

Conservatives place greatest value on the original meaning of the text itself. 'Strict constructionism' and 'originalism' are among the two best known: the former emphasises the literal meaning of the text; the latter, whose most high-profile exponent is Antonin Scalia, seeks to establish what a 'reasonable' reading contemporary to the adoption would have been.

There are a number of arguments that underpin the conservative view.
- One of Scalia's maxims is that the constitution is 'dead'; every other law is 'dead' in the sense that its meaning does not change over time, and the constitution is itself nothing more than a particular form of law. If anything, as a statement of fundamental principles, there is more reason to keep the constitution unchanged than any other law.
- A reading contemporary to the framing of the constitution is the most objective standard available; a 'living constitution' approach favoured by liberals means that the constitution simply becomes a reflection of the values of the current justices. It means that the court's judgements are more predictable and stable.
- The framers incorporated a process for amending the constitution and this should be used should the need arise; rights which judges 'find' in the text in controversial areas are likely to be divisive and seen by opponents to lack legitimacy, as has been the case with the constitutional right to abortion created by *Roe* v *Wade*.

Liberal approaches

Liberals give less value to the strict meaning of the constitution and more to the outcomes of the court's decisions. Often liberal approaches are linked with the term 'living constitution', which conveys the idea that the constitution has to be interpreted to make it relevant to modern society.

There are a number of arguments that underpin the liberal view.
- The constitution was written in broad terms, as the framers themselves envisaged the need for it to evolve and included deliberately vague terms such as the 'general welfare' to enable this to happen.
- The framers misjudged the amendment process to the constitution; the requirement of two-thirds majorities in Congress, and approval by three-quarters of the state legislatures is too demanding, so that it becomes the responsibility of the court to bring the constitution up to date.
- Society's values change; when the constitution was framed, for example, a variety of punishments such as public flogging were considered acceptable, and it would be ludicrous to insist on retaining the framers' view of 'cruel and unusual punishments'.
- 'Originalism' is too inflexible and not even applied consistently by originalists themselves. For example, no originalist justice on the current court has ever publicly criticised the decision in *Brown* v *Topeka Board*, when much of the evidence suggests that the framers of the 14th Amendment (the 'equal protection of the laws' clause, on which the *Brown* decision was based) regarded it as consistent with the existence of segregated schools.

> **Knowledge check 52**
>
> Why is it unlikely that any justice would express criticism of the *Brown* decision?

Judicial activism and restraint

Judicial activism and restraint are terms which are probably used more frequently than any others in discussions of the Supreme Court. However, both lack precise definition, and in some contexts become almost meaningless labels of approval (restraint) and disapproval (activism) which are applied by supporters and opponents to every aspect of the court's operation — decisions, individual justices and the character of the span of a court's life (for example, 'the Warren Court'). 'Judicial activism', in particular, often has the function of a catch-all term of disapproval for any decision or individual or court with which a speaker or writer disagrees.

The nearest to an objective definition of **judicial activism** is the overriding by the court of a state or congressional law, or the reversal of one of the court's own precedents. **Judicial restraint** is even less easy to define objectively, since the logical opposite of activism would be inactivism, but no one advocates that the court should be completely inert. Advocates of judicial restraint would argue that the court should only intervene in the most egregious cases of constitutional violation, but the problem of securing agreement over whether any particular case constitutes such a violation is obvious.

Examiner tip

Students are frequently hazy about the meaning of 'judicial activism' and 'judicial restraint'. Particularly if either is a term in the question, make sure you are completely clear before you start writing your response.

The power of the court

Sources of the court's power

- The most significant power of the court is judicial review, the ability to declare both state and federal laws, and the actions of other branches of government, unconstitutional. This effectively gives the court the power to revise the constitution, and become, as Wilson famously said, a 'constitutional convention in continuous session'.
- The other two branches check the court less than they check each other. The court's rulings can be reversed through a constitutional amendment but, given the difficulty of the process, it is unsurprising that only four decisions have been reversed in this way. There have been reversals by the court itself, for example *Brown* reversed *Plessy*, and *Johnson* reversed *Bowers* but, since they hardly bolster faith in the court's judgement, they are only carried out reluctantly. In cases where interpretation of congressional law is at issue, Congress can reverse a decision itself through passage of new legislation; for example, *Ledbetter* v *Goodyear* was reversed by the Equal Pay Act of 2009, the first legislation signed by President Obama.
- Since they are appointed for life, and not accountable to either an electorate or any other institution for their decisions, justices are in theory completely insulated, from public opinion in particular.
- As the range of government activity has expanded, the court's jurisdiction has extended to an increasing proportion of national life; in nearly 170 years from 1787 until 1954 the Supreme Court overruled 77 federal laws, but since then it has already overruled more than 80.

- As de Tocqueville remarked in the nineteenth century, 'Scarcely any political question arises in the United States that is not resolved, sooner or later, into a judicial question'; the litigious nature of American society means that there are few issues which do not become the subject of court cases.

Limits on the court's power

- There are three formal checks in the constitution, none of them particularly meaningful: Congress has the power to vary the size of the court (last tried unsuccessfully by President Roosevelt in 1937), to vary the sorts of case heard by court (used once, just after the Civil War), and to impeach justices (no Supreme Court justice has ever been convicted on impeachment).
- The practical checks on the court are more significant. Although in theory the Supreme Court is insulated from public opinion, in practice justices will be very aware of public reaction to their decisions; if the legitimacy of the court as an unelected body in a democracy is to be maintained, it cannot be seen to be constantly making decisions which run counter to the clear preferences of a majority of the population. This was seen in the aftermath of *Furman* v *Georgia* when, in response to what was effectively a court-created de facto ban on capital punishment, 35 states passed new death-penalty laws. In their judgement 2 years later in *Gregg* v *Georgia*, the court ruled that the death penalty was *not* in all circumstances unconstitutional, and conceded that the 'most marked indication of society's endorsement of death penalty for murder...[was the] legislative response to *Furman*'.
- In addition to the above, the Supreme Court requires the other branches to interpret and implement its decisions. Most famously, the desegregation of schools, which should have occurred as a consequence of the *Brown* decision in 1954, only really got under way in the late 1960s after the passage of congressional legislation, giving the administration the power to withhold federal funds from schools refusing to desegregate.

Debate

Arguments about the legitimacy of the role of the Supreme Court as an unelected body in a democracy are still very current.

Critics on the right argue that, as an unelected body with no effective checks, it should defer to the elected branches, and only overrule them in the most flagrant cases of constitutional violation. Otherwise, the court may be viewed as endorsing a particular political viewpoint as 'constitutional' — for example, in its striking-down of the New Deal legislation of the 1930s — and consequently undermine its own legitimacy. If some parts of the constitution *are* ambiguous, then, since it is impossible to show a clear violation, this should act as a brake on the expansion of judicial review; instead, in the hands of liberals, it has become the pretext for it. Furthermore, judges are expert in law, not social policy, and judge-made social policy is often ineffective and unworkable in practice. The *Roe* trimester framework, for example, was abandoned by the court in its *Casey* ruling.

Liberals argue that the combination of a separated system of government and risk-averse politicians means that legislation in contentious areas is unlikely to be passed

Knowledge check 53

What is the *Roe* trimester framework?

and that, if the court does not act, access to basic rights could be denied indefinitely. Further, cases such as *Plessy* v *Ferguson* show that, if the court is willing to overturn only the most flagrant breaches of the constitution, injustices will persist. In practice, constitutional amendments *have* been used to check the power of the court: the 16th Amendment overruled the decision in *Pollock*, for example.

A 'hollow hope'?

Some have argued (for example, Gerald Rosenberg in *The Hollow Hope*) that the failure of *Brown* in bringing about desegregation of schools, and its relatively minor role in the wider Civil Rights movement, suggests that the Supreme Court is very far from the 'imperial judiciary' that its opponents depict. Likewise, *Roe* v *Wade* may only have been one factor in the expansion of abortion rights, and has not necessarily been a positive factor in their retention. By the early 1970s, the climate around abortion was changing, before *Roe* was decided. The number of abortions was already increasing, and several states had already reduced their restrictions on abortion. The impact of *Roe* was then subsequently limited by executive and legislative action, such as the Hyde amendment which was reaffirmed by President Obama in 2010. In many states, abortion provision is now so limited that it is hardly any better than if *Roe* had never happened; the controversial nature of the decision in *Roe* galvanised opponents, and it could be argued that a more incremental, state-based approach would have been more successful in advancing the cause of abortion rights.

A political body?

The centrality of the role of the Supreme Court in the political system has led to a debate over whether it should more appropriately be seen as a political rather than a judicial body.

There are a number of arguments that underpin the view that the court is a *political* body:

- Justices are nominated and confirmed by politicians. It is accepted that a president will nominate a candidate sympathetic to his agenda, and nominees will come to the confirmation process with a track record of judgements and/or writings indicative of their ideological perspective.
- Justices are increasingly divided along ideological lines in their decision making.
- The power of the court through judicial review to declare the laws and actions of the elected branches unconstitutional inevitably gives its role a political element.
- The court is used by political actors, particularly interest groups, for political ends; groups sponsor test cases and lobby the court through amicus curiae briefs.
- The judgement process itself is political. In the process of reaching a decision, justices will try to ensure their view prevails; they will form alliances against opponents, strike bargains and offer compromises.
- Judgements are not arrived at in a judicial vacuum; judges are aware of public opinion and the likely impact of their decisions.

Knowledge check 54

What is meant by the term 'imperial judiciary'?

Knowledge check 55

What was the Hyde amendment?

The integrity of the court as a *judicial* body is defended by the following:

- Justices would claim to be 'neutral umpires', as did the current Chief Justice in his confirmation hearings.
- Many cases are decided by purely technical and legal considerations, and only a few high-profile cases have overtly political implications.
- Judges are constrained by precedent, which they are reluctant to overturn, and by the law itself.
- Justices may rule against their own stated preferences — for example, Justice Kennedy, in the *Texas v Johnson* judgement, wrote: 'The hard fact is that sometimes we must make decisions we do not like. We make them because they are right, right in the sense that the law and the constitution, as we see them, compel the result.'

The Roberts Court

Background

John Roberts assumed the role of Chief Justice in 2005 and is only the fourth to hold the title since 1953. Roberts was preceded as Chief Justice by William Rehnquist. The Rehnquist Court began its life in 1986 with the nomination of Rehnquist by Ronald Reagan to replace the then Chief Justice, Warren Burger, a Nixon appointee. The composition of the Rehnquist Court remained unchanged from 1993 until Roberts' appointment in 2005, an unusually lengthy period. It was divided into a solidly conservative bloc of Rehnquist, Scalia and Thomas; a solidly liberal bloc of Stevens, Souter, Ginsburg and Breyer; and two less clearly aligned justices, Kennedy and Day O'Connor.

Since Roberts took over from Rehnquist, the composition of the court has changed fairly markedly, with three further members of the Rehnquist Court stepping down. Of the three replacements, the nomination of Samuel Alito has been widely seen as the most significant, since Alito replaced Sandra Day O'Connor who, although a nominee of President Reagan, was only conservative in a proportion of her views. Alito was expected, and has proved to be, much more consistently conservative, and this has meant that there are now two blocs of four consistent conservatives and four consistent liberals, leaving Kennedy as the only justice not unequivocally identified with either one of them.

The Roberts Court initially consisted of seven Republican nominees to only two Democratic; Alito was a Republican nominee replacing a Republican nominee, but since the appointment of Sonia Sotomayor and Elena Kagan by President Obama, the partisan balance has shifted from 7–2 to 5–4. However, since the Republican-nominated justices they replaced, David Souter and John Paul Stevens, were on the liberal wing, the ideological balance has been unaffected.

Composition of the Roberts Court

Antonin Scalia (1986) — an appeals court judge for 4 years prior to his nomination, Scalia's judicial reputation preceded him and he was confirmed 98–0. He became the longest-serving member of the court with the resignation

Texas v Johnson Gregory Johnson was a political activist who burnt an American flag in the course of a march in Dallas in 1984. He was convicted of desecrating the flag in violation of Texas law, but his conviction was overturned on appeal, both in Texas and by the Supreme Court, on the grounds that flag burning is protected by the First Amendment.

of John Paul Stevens in 2009, and is widely regarded as the leading conservative intellect on the court.

Anthony Kennedy (1988) — the second Reagan nominee on the court, Kennedy was the third-choice nominee after the defeat of the nomination of Robert Bork and the withdrawal of Douglas Ginsburg. Kennedy was a much less controversial nomination than his two predecessors and was confirmed 97–0. He is generally but not reliably conservative, and wrote, for example, the majority opinion in *Lawrence* v *Texas* in 2003. He is the nearest thing to a 'swing justice' on the current court, and his power to move a decision in the direction of either the liberal or conservative bloc of four have led some commentators to speak of the 'Kennedy Court'.

Clarence Thomas (1991) — along with the rejection of Robert Bork, Thomas's confirmation hearings were the most controversial episode in the recent history of the court. Thomas was given only a 'qualified' rating by the ABA, and the further controversy of the appearance of Anita Hill led to almost the narrowest possible confirmation vote of 52–48.

Ruth Bader Ginsburg (1993) — the second woman justice to be appointed after Sandra Day O'Connor in 1981, Ginsburg had served as an appeal court justice for 13 years prior to her nomination. Her voting record on the appeals court characterised her as a moderate liberal, and she was reportedly recommended for the nomination in 1993 by the Republican senator Orrin Hatch. This combination probably contributed to her near unanimous confirmation vote of 96–3.

Stephen Breyer (1993) —the second nominee of President Clinton, he had served on the First Circuit Court of Appeal since 1980. His nomination was uncontroversial and he was confirmed by the Senate 87–9. Although unambiguously identified with the liberal bloc of the court, his judicial approach is often characterised as pragmatic and cautious, and a *New York Times* survey of 2005 found that he had voted to overturn congressional law less frequently than any other member of the Rehnquist Court.

John Roberts (2005) — the current Chief Justice, he was confirmed 78–22. Every Republican senator voted in support, and he split the then 44 Democratic senators exactly 50:50. His passage through the confirmation hearings was particularly smooth; he had been a judge only for a short while since 2003, and had only a sparse track record of judgements or pronouncements for opponents to work with. He proved to be an accomplished performer in front of the committee and showed a detailed command of constitutional law. As a conservative replacing the conservative Chief Justice William Rehnquist, he was not seen as changing the balance of court, and was sufficiently conciliatory, for example, in describing *Roe* as 'settled precedent', to avoid giving opponents ammunition.

Samuel Alito (2006) — as an appeal court judge since 1990, Alito was more obviously qualified than Miers, who he was brought in to replace after the withdrawal of her nomination, but a more controversial choice than Roberts. As a new judge on the Third Circuit Court of Appeals, he had been the lone

Knowledge check 56

What is a 'swing justice'?

Knowledge check 57

What is the ABA? Why are its ratings significant?

dissenter in a 1991 decision striking down the requirement of a Pennsylvania law that required women to inform their husbands before being permitted to have an abortion. In addition, as a replacement for Sandra Day O'Connor, he was seen as significantly altering the balance of the court. However, he was helped by the Democrats on the committee, who were criticised in the press for the verbose and tangential style of their interrogation, and his own responses were sufficiently guarded to avoid generating any further controversy.

Sonia Sotomayor (2009) — like Alito, Sotomayor had a long record as an appeals court judge prior to nomination, having been appointed to the Second Circuit court in 1998. She was described by the White House as bringing 'more federal judicial experience to the Supreme Court than any justice in 100 years' and there was little controversy in her hundreds of rulings. The only significant source of concern for her supporters was her widely reported comment that 'a wise Latina woman with the richness of her experiences would more often than not reach a better conclusion than a white male who hasn't lived that life'. She was able to explain it as 'a rhetorical flourish that fell flat...'. Despite her (what seemed to many) obvious merits, she was confirmed by the relatively narrow margin of 68–31, with only ten Republicans voting to support her, a notable contrast with the level of Democratic support for John Roberts only 4 years previously.

Elena Kagan — Kagan was the first non-judge to be confirmed for 38 years. Prior to nomination, there were few indications of her views on controversial issues, and she was described in the *Washington Post* as having the 'extraordinary ability, while holding high-profile jobs in the legal profession, to say nothing on the major issues of the day'. Because of this lack of a track record, she was seen somewhat in the same light by some on the left as Harriet Miers had been seen by conservatives, although her legal credentials were much stronger. It was also not in her favour that she would further concentrate the geographical bias of the court towards New York, as she would be the fourth New York judge appointed, including all three women. Nevertheless, her assured handling of the confirmation interviews meant that there was little doubt that she would be confirmed, although only by 63 votes to 37, with just five Republicans supporting her, even fewer than had voted for Sotomayor.

Ideological direction

With John Roberts installed as Chief Justice since 2005, commentators have sought to identify the ideological direction of the Roberts Court. A number of the court's decisions have caused controversy and probably none more than two decisions of 2010, *Citizens United v FEC* and *Heller* v *DC*. First, both were a clear endorsement of conservative values: the right of corporations to involve themselves in election campaigns in *Citizens United*, and the rights of gun owners in *Heller*. Second, in both the court found congressional legislation unconstitutional: in the case of *Citizens United*, a federal law, and in the case of *Heller*, a federal law applicable only to Washington DC; *Citizens United* also saw the reversal of an earlier court decision, *McConnell* v *FEC*.

Citizens United v FEC
This case resulted in probably the single most controversial decision of the Roberts Court. It struck down the regulation of 'issue ads' contained in the Bipartisan Campaign Reform Act of 2002, and means that corporations and unions are now free to spend unrestricted funds on political ads throughout campaigns.

Knowledge check 58

Why has the Roberts Court been described as 'activist conservative'?

For many commentators, especially on the left, these decisions signalled the arrival of an 'activist' conservative court, distinctly at odds with the moderate and neutral image that Roberts had conveyed at his confirmation hearing. The Roberts Court has shown itself to be even more sceptical than its predecessor in its treatment of race-based programmes and approaches; in *Ricci* v *DeStefano* and *Meredith* v *Jefferson County Board of Education*, the court rejected favourable treatment for minorities and the use of race in school place allocations as a means of social engineering.

However, the direction of any court will rarely be unambiguously one way. Some of its more controversial decisions, which have been at odds with significant sections of public opinion, have been supported across ideological lines; for example, a series of decisions have upheld 1st Amendment rights of freedom of expression in cases such as *Snyder* v *Phelps*. The liberal bloc has not been entirely unsuccessful, particularly in the area of sentencing and the death penalty; in the decision in *Graham* v *Florida* in 2010, for example, the liberals were joined by both Kennedy and Roberts in declaring that a sentence of life without parole for juveniles for offences not involving murder should be regarded as cruel and unusual.

Looking to the future, given the composition of the court, and particularly the conservative tendencies of Justice Kennedy, it would be surprising if the conservative bloc did not continue to have the upper hand. However, whether this will extend to the achievement of some of the most cherished goals of the conservative movement, such as the reversal of *Roe* v *Wade*, remains to be seen.

Summary

- As the self-appointed guardian of the constitution, the role of the Supreme Court has been controversial throughout its life.

- The appointment process requires nomination by the president and confirmation by the Senate; in recent years the Senate's role has been criticised for excessive partisanship.

- The fundamental divide between the justices on the court is over approaches to judicial interpretation, and the extent to which the original meaning of the constitution should be adhered to.

- Originally seen as the 'least dangerous' branch, the court's power of judicial review is almost uncheckable by any other part of the US system.

- The extent of the court's involvement in the political system has given rise to a debate over the extent to which it can be regarded as a purely judicial body.

- The ideological direction of the Roberts Court is still emerging, but some of its most consequential decisions have been clearly conservative.

Questions & Answers

At the beginning of this section there is an explanation of the assessment objectives and a guide as to how the marks for each assessment objective are distributed among the different questions on the paper. There follow some specimen examination questions. These are neither past examination questions, nor future examination questions, but they are very similar to the kind of questions you will face.

The best way to use this section of the guide is to look at each question and make notes on how you would go about answering it, including the key facts and knowledge you would use, relevant examples, the analysis, arguments and evaluations you would deploy and the conclusions you would reach. You should also make a plan of how you would answer the whole question, taking into account the examiner tip (indicated by the icon ⓔ immediately below the question.

After each specimen question there are two exemplar answers. One will be a strong answer and the other will be either weak or of medium quality. The strength of each specimen answer is indicated in the examiner commentary (again indicated by the icon ⓔ that follows it. In the commentary there are also notes on the answer's strengths and weaknesses and an indication as to how marks would be awarded for each assessment objective. Now compare these specimen answers with your own notes. Amend your notes to bring them to the standard of the stronger specimen. Having done all this, you can now attempt a full answer to the question, aiming to avoid the weaknesses and include the strengths that have been indicated in the specimen answers and explanations of the marks.

Of course you may use the information in your own way. The above guidance is merely a recommendation. Remember, however, that simply 'learning' the strong specimen answers will not help — these are answers to specimen questions, not to the questions you will actually face. It is preferable to learn how to answer questions 'actively', that is by writing your own answers, using the questions and answers as a guide. In this way you will be able to tackle effectively any questions that may come your way in the examination.

Assessment guidance

Assessment objectives overview

	AO1 Knowledge and understanding	AO2 Analysis and evaluation	Synopticity	AO3 Communication and coherence	Total
Short answer	5 marks	7 marks		3 marks	15 marks
Essay question	12 marks	12 marks	12 marks	9 marks	45 marks

Knowledge and understanding

Assessment objective 1 assesses the extent of candidates' knowledge, i.e. what they know relevant to the question.

Analysis and evaluation

Assessment objective 2 is assessing what candidates can do with their knowledge; how far they can analyse it and assess its significance ('micro' evaluation), and how far they can use it to construct a coherent argument ('macro' evaluation).

Synopticity

Synoptic marks are only awarded for essay questions; they assess how far candidates show awareness of competing viewpoints on a particular issue. For some issues, these viewpoints will be ideologically based but, for others, there is no ideological basis worth mentioning. For example, if the question is about the role of the Supreme Court, there are clearly defined conservative and liberal positions and it would be advisable for candidates to refer to these. However, if the question is asking how far Congress remains a powerful body, candidates are being asked to weigh up competing sets of evidence, and here it would not be helpful to try and identify conservative and liberal positions.

Communication and coherence

Assessment objective 3 assesses the extent to which candidates can organise points in a logical sequence and can sustain a clear and coherent line of argument throughout.

Short-answer guidance

There are a number of basic guidelines for short answers:
- An introduction is unnecessary; you are not advancing an argument, so just go straight into your first point.
- For 'to what extent' questions, make sure you cover *both* sides raised by the question.
- Only do what the question asks. For example, if it asks for criticisms of the process of appointing Supreme Court justices, do not give justifications as well.
- Aim for about three or, ideally, four well-developed points.

Essay guidance

There are a number of basic guidelines for essay answers:
- Essay questions will *always* invite you to discuss two sides of an issue; ensure you cover them, and give roughly equal space to each.
- You need an introduction, where you sketch out the nature of the debate and indicate the direction your argument will be following.
- Make it clear throughout the essay which side of the debate you are supporting; do not leave it until the conclusion to announce the 'winner'.
- The simplest structure is to look at one side of the debate in the first half of the answer and the other in the second.
- Keep focused on the key terms of the question, for example 'the power to persuade'; do not allow yourself to drift into a general discussion of, for example, presidential power.
- You need a conclusion, in which you restate the main points of your argument.

Question 1 **The constitution**

What are the benefits and drawbacks of the process of amending the constitution?   (15 marks)

🄮 This is a straightforward question and the simplest approach is to answer it in two consecutive halves — benefits and drawbacks. Nothing more elaborate is required. It is important to be clear on exactly what the terms of the question mean; here, for example, the process refers to the formal process by which the constitution is amended, and it would not be relevant to bring in the role of the Supreme Court.

Student A

There are two processes by which the US Constitution can be amended, although only one has ever been used. This is when a proposed amendment is passed with two-thirds majorities in both chambers of Congress and is then approved by three-quarters of state legislatures. To date there have been 27 amendments, although ten of these were the Bill of Rights, which some have argued were simply an omission from the original drafting, and two of the amendments concerning prohibition have cancelled each other out.

🄮 A very confident start. The accurate knowledge of the formal process of amendment is clearly rewardable, and the historical knowledge creates a context for the points which are to follow.

A considerable benefit of this method is that it requires tremendous broad-based democratic support. Amendments cannot, as is the case in some countries, simply be passed by the national legislature; rather they must consult the regional powers — the state legislatures. This means that the people will have multiple opportunities to have their voices heard in the amendment process, at both a national and state level. This therefore ensures that any amendment has genuine and substantial democratic support.

🄮 This point is relatively obvious, but it is particularly well explained.

Moreover, given that any proposed amendment will be considered at two levels, it is clear that it will be subject to considerable scrutiny and therefore more likely to prove effective. It is significant to note that only 27 amendments have been passed in 200 years, guaranteeing that the core principles of the constitution, which are almost universally approved of, will remain intact.

🄮 This is really two points, and the second could be explained a little more fully, in particular the phrase 'almost universally approved of', which leaves several questions hanging in the air.

A final benefit of this process is that proposed amendments do not, unless stipulated, have time limits. This was most notable in the 27th Amendment, which was actually proposed in the eighteenth century. This means, therefore, that if an idea is worthy of approval it will have a significant chance to gain approval over time.

ⓔ This is not an obvious point and it is a good example first of the student knowing a relatively obscure detail of the amendment process, and second of their thinking on their feet to make what they know relevant to the question.

However, it is important to recognise there are drawbacks too. Foremost among these is a difficulty of the process which, while it ensures that certain basic principles will be protected, it also means that 'today's generation will be limited by the political inhibitions of their forefathers' **a**. This may well mean that the constitution is made increasingly irrelevant by its inability to adapt to modern politics and life **b**.

ⓔ **a** Quotations can be effective, but they receive no extra credit, and often it is simpler and less effort to express the same thought in your own words. **b** This is a rewardable point but it would be stronger if there was an example given of the constitution's inability to adapt.

Additionally, the nature of the process leaves power in the hands of politicians, which can mean that amendments the people want are not passed. A poll for the *New York Times* found that 63% of Americans supported the Equal Rights Amendment **c**, but it failed to receive the support of the required number of state legislatures. Thus in this instance the nature of the process meant that the political will of the nation was ignored **d**.

ⓔ **c** Statistics in an examination answer invariably look made up, and although this student at least quotes a source, this percentage is not an exception. **d** The history of the ERA is certainly relevant to this answer, but it would be better if it was explained in a way which did not make it a straight contradiction of the point in the second paragraph. Despite one or two weaknesses, overall this is a strong answer and would receive an A grade in the exam.

ⓔ **13/15 marks awarded.**

Student B

In order to amend the constitution of the United States a majority vote in Congress is required, along with the ratification of 75% of the states.

A benefit of this system is that it involves good scrutiny. The need for a supermajority in Congress of two-thirds means that the amendments will be checked thoroughly by numerous specialists. The fact that there have only ever been 27 shows how the scrutiny of an amendment is effective, along with the fact that so many fall, for example the Balanced Budget Amendment and Flag Desecration Amendment. The process to amend the constitution clearly allows for scrutiny, which was the intention of the Founding Fathers.

ⓔ The point about scrutiny is rewardable but it is not really explained what the proposed amendments are scrutinised for, and it is not convincingly supported by the two examples of failed amendments.

Additionally, the process is positive as it allows for the constitution to change over time to protect rights. The context of American society has entirely changed since the constitution was written and so the process of amendment allows updates depending on this change. For example, the Bill of Rights has increased personal liberties of the increasing population and after 100 years the 13th, 14th and 15th Amendments finally gave African Americans civil liberties.

(e) Again, this is a rewardable point, but it is saying little more than that the constitution can change, and it is not specifically linked to the details of the process.

However, a disadvantage is that it can cause controversy and mistakes to occur. This occurred with the passing of the 18th Amendment, which banned alcohol. It caused a rise in the black market, economic decline and rising unemployment, and later had to be repealed. The process can, as a result, be seen to allow for mistakes and controversies that later lead to embarrassment for the constitution.

(e) The history of the Prohibition amendments is highly relevant to this question and this is a rewardable point. Overall this answer makes three rewardable points but none particularly well, and it would receive a C grade in the exam.

(e) **7/15 marks awarded.**

Question 2 **Congress**

Why does Congress pass so few laws? (15 marks)

ⓔ This is another straightforward question. It requires students to analyse the reasons for the small number of laws passed by Congress. The simplest and most effective way is to look at each in turn.

Student A

Although thousands of bills are placed in the hopper in the House of Representatives and on the desk in the Senate each year **a** relatively few make it to law. The reasons for this are the Founding Fathers created a deliberately difficult process because they wanted to limit the size, scope and activity of government **b**.

ⓔ **a** There is nothing wrong with this sort of detail but it gains no extra reward and in an exam every second is important. **b** It is a persistent belief among students that the legislative process is part of the constitution when in fact it says nothing about it.

The first stage is called the first reading — this is merely a formality and there is no debate or vote on the bill. The next stage is the committee stage and this is extremely important. It is conducted by permanent policy specialist committees who have full power of amendment and life or death of the bill. They kill or pigeonhole literally thousands of bills every year and only those with a good deal of support from the administration or the public will go on.

ⓔ This answer is in the form of a narrative, which is certainly rewardable, but it would be stronger if it was more sharply analytical.

After this stage the bill must be returned to the floor of each house. The House rules committee has considerable power over when a bill appears and if they give it a low priority its chances of passing decline. In the Senate a bill may be filibustered, which again reduces its chances. If the two houses produce two different versions of a bill then it has to go to a conference committee, which is again another opportunity for it to fail.

   Finally the president has to sign a bill before it can become law, and he may choose to veto it which is difficult for Congress to reverse.

ⓔ This answer shows a quite detailed and accurate knowledge of the legislative process. However, there are no supporting examples and the narrative approach means that points are made more as asides than as the focus of a paragraph. It would probably just get a B grade in the exam.

ⓔ **8/15 marks awarded.**

Every year over 10,000 bills are proposed, however only a small percentage, usually less than 5%, become law. There are a number of reasons for this.

   First, and most significantly, bills must be passed through both chambers; both have equal power and neither can enforce its will on the other. This often means that not only different bills are produced but sometimes bills are only given priority in one of the two houses. Frequently the House will pass bills which the Senate is reluctant to act on, as happened with Obama's energy bill, and this situation of course is more likely to occur if the two chambers are under the control of different parties, as is the case now.

ⓔ This is a confident and well-explained point, supported by recent evidence.

Another reason that a small percentage of bills are passed is due to the constitutional check of the presidential veto. This is a particularly potent power when Congress and the executive are controlled by different parties, which is so often the case due to split-ticket voting. Of course Congress can override the presidential veto but rarely does a party have the two-thirds majority necessary in Congress and so it depends on there being a bipartisan majority. This occurred when Wilson's veto on the Volstead Act was overridden.

ⓔ The student has made a slightly eccentric choice of example, when there are much more recent vetoes to choose from, but it is a valid one nevertheless.

A further reason that only a small percentage of proposed bills become law is that there is a deliberately long system for passing laws. The committee stage represents a particular difficulty as committee chairmen have the power to pigeonhole a bill, which means it never reappears. In the Senate the filibuster is used increasingly frequently and since 60 votes are needed to break a filibuster, again it almost always requires bipartisan support **a**. Bearing in mind the fact that a congressional session is only 2 years long, if a bill is not passed into law in this time, it dies.

ⓔ **a** Rather than narrate the legislative process as the first answer did, this answer picks out a couple of key stages, which is a stronger approach.

Finally, increased partisanship in Congress has also made it harder to pass bills. Since 2008 nearly all of Obama's legislation has been unanimously opposed by Republicans in both houses, and since a few members of his own party will invariably oppose it as well, because they represent districts with a conservative tendency, it becomes very difficult to assemble the necessary votes. However, it should be pointed out that with the exception of the energy bill, all of Obama's legislative priorities did get passed.

ⓔ This paragraph shows a quite sophisticated knowledge of the dynamics of Congress.

In conclusion it is clear that there are many obstacles in the way of bills making it to law, such as the presidential veto, the dualistic nature of Congress and the fact that the executive and legislature are rarely controlled by the same party.

 This is quite an impressive answer; four points are made, explained in detail and nearly all are supported by evidence. Although there will always be areas which could be improved, it is a clear A grade and probably does enough to get full marks.

(e) 15/15 marks awarded.

Question 3 **The presidency**

Is the president confined to the 'power to persuade'?   (45 marks)

This is a variant of a very standard question on the power of the president. Students need to consider the different areas of the president's power, and how far, if at all, they are dependent on his ability to persuade others to do what he wants.

Student A

The claim that the power of the president is confined to the power to persuade can be challenged in a number of ways. First is that the president has more than only having the power to persuade. And the other the president is confined to more than one thing, the power to persuade included.

This is not an effective introduction, although it is not untypical. It gives no indication of why the 'power to persuade' might be the subject of debate, or where the writer is going to argue that the weight of evidence lies, both of which it should ideally cover.

The president is limited to the power to persuade. For example, the president cannot propose a bill in Congress, for him to get a proposal through he will need to persuade a sympathetic member of both the House of Representatives and the Senate. Once that proposal has gone through, the president will again have to persuade members of Congress to vote in favour. President Obama tried very hard to persuade members in Congress to get his healthcare bill through, however in the end he was subject to making a compromise on limiting abortion. Presidents do not have that much power and the power to persuade is the only major strength they have to help them. Former president LBJ was seen to be the best at persuading, this helped him to push bills quickly through Congress.

Everything that the president does he needs to persuade in order for it to happen. In order for his nominees for appointments to take their position, the president needs not only to persuade Congress but also committees. Although, to many, the powers of the president may be seen to be growing, in reality the only formal power the president holds is the power to persuade.

These two paragraphs make a number of rewardable points. The need for the president to persuade members of Congress to vote for his legislation is clearly relevant, and a recent example from the Obama administration is cited in support. However, the exposition has a very basic quality; nothing is really developed or explored, and for a first half of the essay it is distinctly thin.

However, the claim that the power of the president is confined to the power to persuade can be challenged, as the president holds many positions and with these positions come power. The president is the head of state, with this the president has control on a number of things. As head of state, the president is able to issue signing statements, meaning he can comment on a bill. The president also has the power to veto any bill put forward by Congress. If the president wants something to happen but is stopped by Congress, the president can issue an executive order, meaning that with the help of a department the president does not have to consult Congress. Although as Chief Commissioner **a** the president does not have the power to declare war, the president still does and sends his troops. Congress are reluctant to withdraw the troops as they do not want to undermine the morale of the president. As head of party, in reality the president holds the most power and control over his party, making most decisions made by him and also being supported by the majority of his party **b**.

e **a** As long as it is clear what is meant, it is not a disaster if terms like 'commander-in-chief' are misremembered. **b** This paragraph, which constitutes the entire second half of the essay, is fuller than the first half, in that there are five separate sources of the president's power mentioned. However, they are very much just mentioned; there is no supporting evidence, and no discussion of how significant each has been for recent presidents.

In conclusion, although it may look as if the only power that the president has is the power to persuade, as all they have ever being doing in trying to persuade to get their things in their favour. However looking past that, the power of the president is not only confined to the power to persuade, they have more power and because the president holds such important positions they are able to have a high level of control, increasing their power even more.

e The conclusion attempts to round up what has preceded it, although it is not helped by the mangled quality of the prose. It does though give a verdict on the question, which is more or less justified by the evidence which had been advanced, although it would help if that was briefly referred to. Overall, this student has shown a clear awareness of what the question is about and made some relevant points on both sides of the debate. The answer is thin on content, though, and such content as there is given minimal development. It would receive a C grade in the exam.

e **22/45 marks awarded:** 6/12 for AO1, 5/12 for AO2, 6/12 for synopticity, 5/9 for AO3.

Student B

The constitution invested all executive power in the president, which is outlined in Article 2 of the constitution. The argument over whether the president's power only consists of the power to persuade arises from the extensive set of checks and balances and the separation of powers which frequently impede his ability to carry out his role. In this essay, however, I will argue that although the president's power may be limited in significant ways, it would be misleading to claim that his power consists solely of the power to persuade, especially in relation to his conduct of foreign policy.

e This is a confident introduction, which signals to the reader that the student has a sure grasp of the debate and helpfully, both for themselves and the reader, indicates the line of argument they are proposing to take.

It is certainly true that the president works under significant checks from the other branches. To begin with, he has to get any legislation he wants passed through Congress. Even when both houses of Congress are controlled by the president's own party, they may not be willing to pass his proposals as he wants them, or to pass them at all. The separation of powers means that they do not rely on the president's success to get re-elected themselves, so they have to be persuaded that their interests coincide with his. Bush had to rely on Democratic support to pass his No Child Left Behind education bill, and Obama's healthcare bill came out without the public option which he wanted. At least he did better than Clinton, whose attempt to reform healthcare never got even to a vote in Congress, despite the fact that both houses of Congress had a majority of his own party.

(e) This point is very clearly explained and draws on three different examples to illustrate it.

All the president's appointments and treaties have to be ratified by the Senate and it is by no means automatic that they will be passed, especially treaties which require a two-thirds majority and therefore will always require bipartisan support. Again, senators have to be persuaded that their interests and specifically their re-election will be boosted by voting the way the president wants them to. Recent history shows how difficult both can be for the president; Bush seemed to think that he had earned sufficient political capital to nominate who he liked to the Supreme Court in 2005 but was rudely awakened when his nominee Harriet Miers was forced to withdraw after senators were unimpressed by her knowledge of constitutional law. His father had a similar experience with his nomination of Clarence Thomas, who was widely seen as unqualified, and he barely managed to persuade the Senate that Thomas was worthy of a place on the court. Clinton's Test Ban Treaty was defeated by the Senate in 1999 and although Obama managed to get the START treaty passed in 2010, it took a formidable lobbying effort by almost the entire administration to achieve it, and then it got through only narrowly.

(e) Again, this paragraph contains a good range of examples, which show how a variety of different outcomes may follow the president's attempts at persuasion.

However, despite these limitations, there is a strong argument that the president has a lot more power than simply persuading Congress to pass his legislation and confirm his appointments and treaties. To begin with, he has the negative power of the veto. The president can stop Congress advancing any initiatives congressional leaders might come up simply through vetoing them, and recent presidents have been very willing to veto measures passed by Congress controlled by the opposition party. The attempts by Democrats to attach a timeline for withdrawal from Iraq to continued funding of the campaign met with complete failure, and should the president want to avoid the potentially negative publicity a veto might attract, he can issue a signing statement instead which can have almost the same effect. Bush used signing statements to refuse parts of bills which he claimed infringed his constitutional powers.

(e) An example of a signing statement would have supported the final point, but again a very clear explanation of the points being made, and 'however' clearly signals the change in the direction of the argument.

As commander-in-chief the president has the enumerated power of the sword. In theory only the Congress has the right to declare war but many times in recent years the president has initiated military campaigns without congressional approval or even the knowledge of Congress, as when President Nixon conducted a secret bombing campaign in Cambodia. In 2011 Obama sent forces into action in Libya with no involvement from Congress and Congress was powerless to stop him. The War Powers Act was passed in 1973 to put a brake on the president's ability to wage war unilaterally but it has proved completely ineffective, mainly because of the reluctance of congressmen to be seen to affecting the morale of the troops in battle, and no presidential military action has had to be curtailed because of it. It is probably true that the president could not sustain a long-term large-scale military campaign without congressional approval, but presidents have shown themselves able to manipulate Congress into achieving the result they want, as Bush did by calling for a vote on Iraq in October 2002, just before the midterms.

(e) This paragraph not only gives evidence of presidential war-making, but evaluates intelligently the limited effectiveness of the War Powers Act.

The president also has the power of using executive orders which maximise presidential power. The president's executive orders are the equivalent of congressional legislation but do not need to be passed by Congress. Although in theory they are just rules for the executive branch to follow, in practice they can make significant changes in policy, as was seen when Obama used an executive order to reverse Bush's executive order on stem cell research. Admittedly, executive orders can occasionally be limited by Congress, since if Congress is not persuaded of the legitimacy of an order it may refuse the funding necessary to carry it out, as President Obama found when he attempted to close Guantanamo Bay through executive order. Congress refused to fund it because of concerns over where the detainees would be relocated to and the president was forced to climb down, despite having campaigned on the issue in 2008. However, this is very much the exception, and a good proportion of orders do not require funding anyway.

(e) The strength of the argument is enhanced by the willingness of the student to concede that there are exceptions to the point he or she is making.

In conclusion, the president has a number of powers which maximise his effectiveness and suggest that they far exceed the sole power to persuade. His use of executive orders and agreements and his power as commander-in-chief show how expansive his power can be. The power of Congress to check the president and the subsequent need to persuade certainly reduces his power but it would not be accurate to say he is confined to it.

ⓔ This is a strong conclusion to an impressive answer. It advances a line of argument in the introduction, which is then convincingly sustained throughout the essay. The explanations are clear and detailed, and a wide range of supporting evidence is drawn on. There are always additional points which could be made, and style which could be improved, but for an A-level student in 45 minutes, it is hard to see that this answer could be much improved on, and it gains full marks.

ⓔ **45/45 marks awarded:** 12/12 for AO1, 12/12 for AO2, 12/12 for synopticity, 9/9 for AO3.

Question 4 **The Supreme Court**

Should the Supreme Court interpret the constitution in accordance with its original meaning? (45 marks)

ⓔ The focus of this question is the different approaches justices take to interpreting the constitution, and the key term is 'original meaning'. Students will be expected to argue the merits of an approach based on original meaning and contrast them with the other most commonly used approach, one based on a 'living constitution'.

Student A

The debate over whether the Supreme Court should be interpreting the constitution and its amendments by establishing their original meaning is increasingly relevant with judicial review and judicial activism. Conservatives would argue that justices must only interpret the constitution and its amendments by considering what their original meaning was, while liberals maintain that other things must be considered, such as their relevance today, to ensure that the constitution and its amendments remain relevant in American society and politics.

ⓔ The introduction establishes that the student knows the parameters of the debate. The relevance of the references to 'judicial review' and 'judicial activism' is not explained, and the relationship of these terms to the question is unclear; they would probably have better been omitted.

The conservative view is held most vehemently by the Tea Party, who believe in a strict adherence to the constitution at all times. They argue that instead of being objective and trying to understand what the framers of the constitution had in mind, Supreme Court justices are increasingly lacking judicial restraint and frequently set about to further their own political viewpoints. Conservatives argue that Supreme Court justices have no right to do this. Considering that laws have been made by elected branches of government, the justices do not have the legitimacy, because they are appointed rather than elected, to declare these laws unconstitutional, except in the rare case where laws are unquestionably contradicting the constitution.

ⓔ This is a relevant and rewardable paragraph, but it would be stronger if its focus was the key term of the question, 'original meaning', rather than judicial restraint, the meaning of which is left to the reader to infer.

Moreover, they also do not have the constitutional right. Judicial review was not set out in the constitution and while the 1819 Supreme Court case *McCulloh* v *Maryland* said that 'implied powers' exist in the constitution, conservatives argue the authors of the constitution purposefully did not give the Supreme Court excessive power, therefore according to this view, not only is it illegitimate it also directly contradicts the constitution, if the Supreme Court interprets the constitution and its amendments in any way apart from establishing its original meaning.

(e) This is another rewardable point, which is an improvement on the previous one in that 'original meaning' is more clearly in focus. It is not obvious that it is *McCulloh* that the student wants to refer to, but that is a minor slip.

> Moreover, conservatives believe if the Supreme Court does not interpret the constitution by establishing original meaning, it will lead the court to become a policy maker according to what they think to be appropriate rather than objectively. Conservatives argue that Supreme Court justices are experts in law not social policy and any social policy they introduce, such as through *Roe* v *Wade* or *Brown* v *Board* will be inappropriate and not practical. Arguably this was seen with *Brown* v *Board* where perhaps the justice's lack of knowledge as social policy makers meant they were unaware that any legislation overruling *Plessy* v *Ferguson* would be unlikely to be effectively enforced in large parts of America, especially in the South. This 'legislating from the bench' undermines their authority as they are clearly overreaching the power allocated them in the constitution, which would in turn decrease their ability to be seen as the highest court in the land.

(e) This is perhaps the most clearly made of the three points so far, although the example of the implementation of *Brown* does not obviously illustrate the point about social policy, and a better example might be provided by *Roe*.

> On the other hand, those of a liberal perspective would argue that, while the original meaning should be considered, it is also necessary to consider many other factors. Liberals believe that American society was completely different when the constitution was written in 1789 and therefore what was appropriate and relevant then may not be so any more. They would argue that if original meaning was adhered to, discriminatory doctrine, such as allowed for segregation in public education, would remain. This is because elected officials can be slow to overrule archaic legislation because of fear of public backlash during elections. Liberals therefore argue that it is necessary for the court, as justices are not accountable to the public, to take the lead in overruling archaic legislation, even if sometimes it is at the expense of what the constitution originally meant.

(e) The beginning of the counter-argument is clearly signalled by 'On the other hand'. Original meaning is kept well in focus and the point about the timidity of elected politicians is clearly explained.

> Moreover, some liberals argue that it is hypocritical of conservatives to insist that original meaning must always be established, as conservative justices also further their political preferences in their behaviour. For example, the Supreme Court's decision not to take any of the cases which would have questioned whether the Patriot Act and Bush's actions in the aftermath of 9/11 were in accordance with the constitution. Arguably by avoiding these cases, conservative Supreme Court justices were exercising their political preference that, during times of national security, personal liberties can be sacrificed.

ⓔ This point about the inconsistency of originalist justices is rewardable, although the example cited does not strongly support it. The Supreme Court has traditionally deferred to the commander-in-chief, especially in times of crisis. This example relates to the selection of cases, not constitutional interpretation, and the court *did* hear cases relating to the prosecution of the 'War on Terror' from 2006 onwards.

To conclude, while conservatives argue that the Supreme Court must stick to original meaning in its interpretation of the constitution, because it lacks the legitimacy and constitutional power to do differently, the liberal argument seems more relevant today. In certain instances, liberals are right to think that updating the constitution is a good thing, as the document is living. The legacy of liberal decisions is clearly positive for American society and the principles of freedom that the constitution emphasises, and for this reason the Supreme Court must maintain the ability to interpret the constitution and its amendments in a relevant way for today.

ⓔ In the conclusion the student gives a clear indication of which he or she believes is the stronger side of the argument. 'The legacy of liberal decisions' is a phrase that has not appeared in the essay so far, and it would be helpful if it could be explained, and the view that it has been positive for America defended. Overall, this is a strong answer, although there are inaccuracies and places where the explanation could be clearer or more convincingly argued. It engages with the question and demonstrates a good understanding of a demanding topic. It would receive an A grade in the exam.

ⓔ **35/45 marks awarded:** 10/12 for AO1, 9/12 for AO2, 9/12 for synopticity, 7/9 for AO3.

Student B

Some may argue that judicial restraint should be used by the judges on the Supreme Court in order to make it an effective government, as they are an elected branch and the use of judicial activism could be deemed as unconstitutional. Equally it could be considered that it is important to respect the original intention of the founding fathers. However, a more convincing argument is that the Supreme Court at times may wish to use judicial activism in order to rule in the light of modern-day issues that were not considered by the founding fathers.

ⓔ Even more than the first answer, this answer immediately wants to switch the focus of the discussion onto judicial activism and judicial restraint, and 'original intention' (not meaning) gets one mention. That said, the reference to 'modern-day issues' shows the student is aware of the key debate the question is based around.

It could be argued that the Supreme Court should interpret the constitution by taking its literal meaning as exercised through judicial restraint. First, by doing so the court is respecting the original intention of the founding fathers and the entire basis America was built on. For example, in *DC* v *Heller* (2010) the court ruled directly from the 2nd Amendment 'right to bear arms', clearly understanding the original meaning behind the constitution. Furthermore, if the constitution does not mention the particular issue, it should go through an amendment process instead. An example of this would be the 13th Amendment, which banned the slave trade; despite the constitution not mentioning it, the amendment process resolved the issue rather than inferring from the constitution in the way that activism would.

ⓔ There is quite a lot that is garbled here and the two examples are both in different ways problematic, but there are two rewardable points nevertheless.

In addition to this, the Supreme Court is an elected body and there for life, meaning that its ability to infer from the constitution in the light of modern-day issues could arguably be seen as undemocratic, for example, *Roe* v *Wade* in 1973 inferred from the 14th Amendment a right to privacy, in order to allow women to have an abortion. However, in the 14th Amendment it does not mention abortion anywhere and it is undemocratic to allow a group of unelected people to decide such a controversial issue.

ⓔ Like the previous two, this point could be more clearly explained, but the example chosen is stronger this time.

This view is further supported by how traditional activism could be used in an attempt to advance a certain political party. In 2010, *Citizens United* v *FEC* inferred from the 1st Amendment, freedom of speech, a right allowing anyone to donate any amount of money to an election, overturning McCain Feingold. It could be argued that this ruling was deliberate in helping the conservatives, who gained from large business donations.

   Lastly, the primary role of the court is to carry out checks and balances, which is ensured through judicial restraint. In 1998 *Clinton* v *City of New York* banned his use of the line veto by ruling directly from Article 1, section 7 of the constitution. This said that if the president disagrees he must veto the entire bill not just parts of it, which Clinton appeared to be doing.

ⓔ These paragraphs are less convincing, and the connection of the last one in particular to the question has to be worked at by the reader, if it can be found at all.

However, a more convincing argument is that judicial restraint ignores public opinion and it is often judicial activism that is necessary in the twenty-first century. First, by using judicial activism, it rules on modern-day issues, such as abortion, gay rights and affirmative action. These are all current issues that now affect modern life but when the constitution was written in the eighteenth century, they were not considered, hence the need for activism. In 1973 *Roe* v *Wade* allowed abortion, in 1996 *Romer* v *Evans* inferred from the 14th Amendment a right to privacy that gay rights should be upheld and in 2006 *Meredith* v *Jefferson* ruled affirmative action unconstitutional, as it infringed on whites' rights. Without activism, these rights would not be ensured or restraint would simply ignore them.

In addition to this, judicial activism often follows public opinion. The rulings on gay rights, *Romer* v *Evans* (1996), and abortion, *Roe* v *Wade* (1973) all followed the mass feeling of the electorate of the time. Seeing as judicial restraint prevents this, as it only takes the literal meaning of the constitution, a key democratic principle is undermined.

e These two paragraphs are not unrewardable but they would be better if 'original meaning' was more squarely in focus, rather than the constant references to judicial activism and restraint. The claim that the adherence of the judiciary to public opinion is a 'key democratic principle' needs more arguing for than it receives here.

Furthermore, with judicial restraint you can get ridiculous rulings which can affect the entire make-up of society. In 2011 *Snyder* v *Phelps* **a** ruled it constitutional for a far-right extreme and Christian family to protest at the funeral of a gay soldier on the basis of freedom of speech, 1st Amendment. Clearly the actions of the Phelps family were unforgivable, and the fact that judicial restraint as a method upheld their doings highlights how dangerous it can be to take the literal meaning of every amendment, no matter what the circumstance is.

e **a** Given that the verdict in *Snyder* v *Phelps* was almost unanimous, and was supported by all of the liberal bloc on the court, it is not the most obvious case to use to attack originalism.

To conclude, it is a much more convincing argument that judicial activism in the twenty-first century tends to be the better method to use during a Supreme Court ruling. Issues such as abortion and gay rights affect the USA now and seeing as they were not considered when the constitution was written judicial activism is a necessity. Judicial restraint, however, prevents these civil liberties through using strict constructionism and suggests that in the modern world it is an unrealistic basis to judge every court ruling on.

e The conclusion gives a clear answer to the question, although using the student's own favoured terms again.

Overall this is a creditable answer. It could be more obviously focused on the terms of the question; there are passages of marginal relevance and there is often a lack of clarity, but overall it does show an engagement with the key issues of the debate. It would receive a B grade in the exam.

e 24/45 marks awarded: 7/12 for AO1, 6/12 for AO2, 6/12 for synopticity, 5/9 for AO3.

1 James Madison was a Virginian politician who had a principal role in the drafting of the constitution and went on to be both Secretary of State and president.

2 The Federalist Papers were a series of political commentaries by Alexander Hamilton, John Jay and James Madison, written immediately after the Constitutional Convention of 1787, and a justification of its aims.

3 Article 1 is the longest article of the constitution because it details the powers of Congress, which the framers believed needed the most restraining of the three branches.

4 The Bill of Rights was passed by Congress in 1789 and completed the ratification process by 1791.

5 The prohibition amendments prohibited, and then allowed, the manufacture, sale and transportation of alcohol.

6 *United States* v *Eichman* (1990).

7 The Equal Rights Amendment was passed by Congress in 1972.

8 The Great Society programme was a series of measures passed by Congress in the mid-1960s, expanding the federal role in areas such as education and health with the aim of improving the standards of basic services.

9 The Gun-Free School Zones Act makes illegal the possession of a gun on the grounds of a school or within 1,000 feet of one.

10 Terri Schiavo suffered brain damage in 1990 after a heart attack, and lived in a vegetative state for a number of years; a court battle developed between her husband and her parents over whether her feeding tube should be removed, and ultimately it was in 2005.

11 Texas — four seats.

12 Gerrymandering is the redrawing of electoral boundaries into sometimes bizarre-looking shapes to maximise party advantage; its most famous exponent was Governor Gerry of Massachusetts, one of whose redrawings produced (roughly) the shape of a salamander.

13 Senator Barack Obama in 2008, and Representative James Garfield in 1880.

14 President Obama appointed Ray LaHood as Transportation Secretary in 2008.

15 The Contract with America was the national manifesto of most Republican House candidates for the 1994 midterms.

16 The last presidential veto overridden by Congress was in July 2008 of a medicare bill.

17 FEMA is the Federal Emergency Management Agency.

18 President Clinton was impeached on charges of perjury and obstruction of justice.

19 Earmarking is when members of Congress attach to bills measures which relate to projects benefiting their home state; the practice was claimed to have made some contribution to budget deficit problems.

20 A third of senators (i.e. 33 or 34) face re-election in any one election.

21 Congress declared war against Britain in 1812, Mexico in 1845, Spain in 1898, Germany and Austria in 1917, and Japan and Germany in 1941.

22 A trade bill negotiated under fast track must be introduced to both houses of Congress on the first available day, cannot be amended and must be passed within a maximum of 90 days, requiring a simple majority to pass.

23 Congress authorised the invasion of Afghanistan through a congressional resolution on 14 September 2001.

24 Forty-one senators (of the total 100 Senate members) can exercise an effective veto because 60 votes are required to break a filibuster, which halts the progress of the legislation concerned.

25 A party vote is when a party votes together as a bloc.

26 Representatives from districts which voted for John McCain in 2008 would be likely to oppose President Obama's healthcare reforms because they would assume that this would reflect the views of the majority of their constituents.

27 Woodrow Wilson served longer as president, exactly 8 years from March 1913 until March 1921. Roosevelt served 6 months less, from September 1901 until March 1909.

28 The Neutrality Acts were a series of congressional measures passed in the 1930s which aimed to keep the USA out of armed conflicts elsewhere in the world.

29 The Budget and Impoundment Control Act 1974 withdrew the power of the president to refuse to spend money authorised by Congress.

30 The debate over the imperial presidency largely subsided after the inauguration of President Obama because Congress was resistant to many of his proposals.

31 'Pork' is the securing of home-district and home-state benefits from Congress by members of Congress to aid their re-election; the 'Bridge to Nowhere' was a bridge project in Alaska, which was portrayed in the press as a particularly extravagant example.

32 The Massachusetts special election in 2010 was held after the death of Senator Edward Kennedy, a Democrat. Contrary to many expectations, it was won by the Republican candidate, Scott Brown, and reduced the Democratic majority to 59, below the figure required to break a filibuster.

33 Republican Congresses would generally be more supportive of a Republican president than a Democratic Congress of a Democratic president because the Republican Party is stereotypically more homogenous and easier to control.

34 The government shutdowns of the 1990s occurred in November and December 1995, when President Clinton and the Republican Congress were unable to agree a federal budget.

35 The disappointments of the Latino community in the Obama first term lay in his inability to secure any significant measure reforming immigration.

36 Presidential 'coat-tails' are the electoral benefits congressional candidates receive from a popular presidential candidate of their party.

37 The president *can* offer members of Congress jobs in the executive, but the constitution would require them to give up their seats.

38 The 'bully' in 'bully pulpit' means 'good', as in 'Bully for you'.

39 John Bolton's nomination as UN ambassador was allowed to lapse after the election of a Democratic Congress in November 2006.

40 'Czars' are the heads of units in the EOP.

41 President Truman wanted to nationalise the steel mills to prevent the war effort in Korea being hampered by strikes in the mills.

42 An 'iron triangle' is an alliance between a congressional committee, an agency or department of the federal bureaucracy, and an interest group formed to promote their mutual interests.

43 John Tower's nomination for Defense Secretary was rejected by the Senate for a number of reasons, including allegations about his personal life and overly close ties with defence contractors.

44 The Israel lobby is the collective term for the pressure groups working to promote the interests of Israel; principal among them is AIPAC (the American Israel Public Affairs Committee).

45 The 'Velcro Veep' was so called because everything, especially bad news, seemed to stick to Dick Cheney during his time as vice-president.

46 Joe Biden complemented Barack Obama because Obama represented a Midwest state, Illinois, and had very limited foreign-policy experience.

47 The Supreme Court has an important role in US politics because the constitution is what the court says it is, and the court has expanded the reach of the constitution to embrace controversial issues such as abortion.

48 Robert Bork was the last Supreme Court nominee rejected by the Senate, in 1987.

49 Anita Hill's appearance caused controversy because she accused Thomas of sexual harassment, and some salacious details emerged in the course of her testimony.

50 Interest groups run ads for and against Supreme Court candidates because the selection of the right (or wrong) candidate is crucial to their cause.

51 Justices are unaccountable because they are unelected and have tenure for life.

52 No justice would express criticism of the *Brown* decision because it is universally regarded as the court's greatest achievement of the twentieth century, if not ever.

53 The *Roe* trimester framework divides the period of pregnancy into three 3-month terms, and the rights of a pregnant woman to abortion vary at each stage.

54 The term 'imperial judiciary' is a variant of the more famous 'imperial presidency', and is used by critics to characterise unfavourably what they see as the excessive power of the Supreme Court.

55 The Hyde amendment was passed in 1977, and banned the use of federal funds for abortion provision.

56 A 'swing justice' refers to a justice who may side with either the liberal or the conservative bloc on the court.

57 The ABA is the American Bar Association; it gives all judicial nominees a rating, ranging from 'not qualified' to 'well qualified', and these are widely reported in the press.

58 The Roberts Court been described as 'activist conservative' because it has reversed earlier court decisions and congressional laws (= 'activism') to the benefit of conservative goals.